# PERSONAL FINANCE

## For Beginners

A Comprehensive Guide on How to Create, Spend,
Save, and Invest Your Money

Aidan Stanford

Title  | PERSONAL FINANCE FOR BEGINNER
         A Comprehensive Guide on How to Create, Spend,
         Save, and Invest Your Money

Author | Aidan Stanford

ISBN  | 9798865024514

*To those who have the courage to embark
on their journey toward financial success.*

# Table of Contents

1. INTRODUCTION ........................................................... 9

2. WHAT MONEY IS ...................................................... 15

   Money's purpose....................................................16

   Evolution of money ...............................................20

   Limited resources and financial choices .................24

   Money-related emotions and perceptions................25

   Money and personal goals......................................27

   Money's role in social structure............................28

3. MONEY GENERATION............................................. 33

   The money cycle....................................................36

   The first opportunity to learn and grow ...............39

   Value creation .......................................................47

   One, two, ...many sources of income ....................50

   Generative Assets: how to create passive income.......54

   Make an investment in yourself.............................56

   Financial planning is crucial ................................57

4. HOW TO SPEND MONEY ....................................... 63

   Financial Priorities................................................65

   Track expenses......................................................70

   Review and adapt .................................................72

   Managing unforeseen expenses..............................76

   Tackle debt wisely ................................................79

   Avoid impulsive spending......................................86

   Look for bargains and discounts............................89

The savings mindset ........................................................................ 96

Cut unnecessary spending ............................................................... 98

Automatic savings strategies ......................................................... 101

Dream, save, achieve .................................................................... 103

Smart savings: from small to large expenses ............................... 109

The jar method .............................................................................. 114

Meeting the challenges of saving .................................................. 116

Financial Instruments .................................................................. 118

The invisible enemy ...................................................................... 122

Insurance for everyday life ........................................................... 124

Protection from economic crises .................................................. 125

Succession planning ..................................................................... 134

5. HOW TO GROW MONEY ..................................... 137

Long-term investments ................................................................. 141

Real estate and property .............................................................. 144

Entrepreneurship and startups ..................................................... 145

Passive income ............................................................................. 147

Opportunities in the digital world ................................................ 150

Plan your financial path ............................................................... 152

6. TEN FINAL TIPS ................................................. 155

Acknowledgements ................................................. 173

# Introduction

Imagine being a player in a complex video game. Every move you make impacts your score and progress in the game. But there's a problem: no one has explained the rules, key points, or winning strategies to you. You find yourself moving blindly, hoping your decisions are right, but often stumbling into obstacles that could have been avoided with proper guidance. Similarly, facing real-life without a solid financial education can be like playing a game without knowing the rules. You're entirely at the mercy of events, without the ability to make informed decisions.

School, which should be responsible for providing essential skills to navigate adulthood and actively participate in society, has a very limited role in educating young people about money usage.

The reason for this lies in the fact that the current education system was designed to meet the needs of the industrial era, which originated in the late 19th century.

Factories required workers who could read, write, and calculate, so the focus was on preparing for specific roles. This model had a negative impact on the cultivation of independent and autonomous minds.

As a result, individuals often learn economic management patterns that have been passed down from generation to generation within their own family context. Financial education within the family primarily relies on practical learning rather than theory. It's a journey that involves imitation and experimentation, often initiated through the allocation of weekly or monthly allowances. This practice-oriented approach can be advantageous as it provides young people with tangible opportunities to learn financial management. However, there is an underlying possibility that this method may perpetuate opinions and behaviors rooted in the past. An example could be the idea that a specific financial instrument is safe or risky, based on limited or outdated knowledge.

To enrich family financial education, it would be beneficial for parents to approach the subject with openness and a positive perspective. This could be achieved through open conversations with children regarding their approaches to money management, offering them up-to-date and accurate information. This approach fosters a broader and more informed view of finances, enabling young people to face economic challenges with greater awareness. The truth is that the family, as we know it, represents a kind of living tradition, an entity that has developed values, habits, and beliefs through past generations that lived through periods of economic instability and poverty, when the emphasis was on survival rather than resource management. These experiences may have created an emotional barrier, making it difficult for parents to openly discuss money with their children. Money might have become a taboo, a topic to be avoided rather than explored.

From childhood, we receive money as gifts for birthdays and holidays, and at that moment, our primary thought is to turn it into games and sweets. Over time, we often find ourselves faced with the choice between immediate gratification and the prudence of saving for the future. However, we rarely receive guidance on which choice is the wisest. With only a basic understanding of financial principles, we thus enter adulthood entirely unprepared to navigate the complex financial decisions that life presents.

In this dynamic, we end up spending more than we can truly afford, accumulating debts through credit cards or loans. Often, though, we are not fully aware of the consequences of such decisions, which can ultimately lead to frustration and insecurity.

When there's a lack of sufficient understanding of how to manage one's finances, it's easy to fall into the habit of overspending, neglecting the importance of saving for emergencies, and building a solid future foundation.

Similarly, limited familiarity with various investment options and their potential earning opportunities often renders us incapable of making well-informed decisions. This deprives us of the opportunity to grow our wealth over time and generate additional sources of income. Moreover, fear of risk often keeps us within the realm of conservative choices, thereby missing out on the returns that bolder investments could offer.

Social pressures contribute to the complexity of the situation. The constant demand to maintain a specific public image and adhere to seemingly high standards of living can add further financial stress to our lives. We are compelled to make decisions that temporarily meet social expectations, often neglecting the long-term sustainability of such choices.

However, amidst these financial and social challenges, we can identify a fundamental anchor: financial planning. This tool not only assists us in avoiding the consequences of impulsive and hasty choices but also serves as an emotional protective system. Like a sturdy umbrella in a torrential downpour, sound financial planning shields us from the unforeseen curveballs that life may throw our way.

Furthermore, financial planning plays a vital role in promoting emotional well-being. It is undeniable that concerns related to financial matters can amplify existing emotional burdens. It is in this context that accurate financial planning plays a crucial role in achieving economic goals as well as becoming a valuable mental tool. By providing us with a greater sense of security and adaptability, this tool helps us face life's challenges with resilience.

Moreover, by aligning our financial decisions with personal values, financial planning provides a solid framework that allows us to approach challenges with greater confidence, thereby contributing to a sense of balance and satisfaction in our financial lives.

When we recognize the interconnectedness between financial stability and mental well-being, we are better prepared to embark on the journey of creating a resilient and enduring financial plan.

The essential importance of providing young people with the tools of financial education becomes evident. This book is specifically designed to fill the gaps that often exist in both school and family education. Its purpose is to guide young individuals in preparing themselves to face the future with greater confidence and competence, preventing the accumulation of financial worries and challenges.

However, this financial journey will not be limited to a series of numbers and strategies; it will also be an opportunity to delve deeper into who you are. Through the learning process, you will explore your emotions, beliefs, and aspirations. You will learn to master not only the world of money but also your mind, becoming a true captain of your financial ship.

So, prepare to cast your nets into the vast ocean of financial opportunities. You will explore concepts such as mindful saving, budget planning, and the art of investments. You will discover how to avoid common traps, escape spending impulses, and build a solid and secure financial future. Begin this journey with an open mind and an insatiable desire for learning. The financial future you deserve awaits you right within the pages of this book.

# Chapter 1

# What money is

*Auri sacra fames.* If there is one thing that has fascinated and plagued humanity since ancient times, it is money. As Virgil said, the insatiable hunger for gold has whetted the ambitions of many people, leading them into a world of possibilities and challenges. But what exactly is money? Reducing the concept to the minutest terms, we could define it as a tool that allows us to exchange goods and services. It is like a kind of magic talisman that allows us to buy whatever we want, from ice cream to the house we live in. It is a symbolic rap-presentation that transcends its material form.

This monetary symbol has no intrinsic value, but it represents the accumulation of resources, skills, and concepts. But its importance goes far beyond the simple exchange of resources. Money has become a symbol of status and power, influencing social dynamics and our sense of identity. By exploring the cultural meaning of money, we will discover how our financial perspectives are shaped by the social and cultural norms of where we live. Our beliefs and values about money can vary widely based on our culture of belonging, influencing our financial decisions.

But money also has a profound impact on our psychology. Our emotions, fears, and aspirations can play a determining role in our financial choices; greed, social influence, and other emotions can push us to take financial actions that may not be rational or beneficial in the long run.

## Money's purpose

Think of a reality in which the concept of money does not exist. In this situation, in order to acquire what you need, it would be necessary to directly exchange the goods and services you own with those offered by other people. This was the primordial system of exchange, used for thousands of years in different cultures and civilizations. However, it had some limitations, as it required a coincidence of needs and offers between the people involved in the exchange. As human communities grew and commercial transactions increased, it became evident that the barter system was inefficient and complicated. This gave rise to the concept of money: as a means of facilitating the exchange of goods and services.

The invention of money, in its many forms, revolutionized commerce and society. It became a universal medium of exchange, accepted by all as a unit of value.

Due to this uniformity of money, people were able to exchange goods and services more easily and more rapidly, improving trade efficiency and smoothness. Instead of having to find a person who has what you need and is willing to take what you offer in exchange, money allows you to convert the value of your goods and services into a form that is easily transferable and accepted by all. You can then use this form of money to get what you need from any other person in society.

This ability of money to serve as a universal medium of exchange has had a revolutionary impact on human society. It has fostered economic growth and the evolution of civilizations, allowing people to specialize in different trades and trade with other per-sons, thus creating a network of interdependence that has alimented the development of communities. Currency plays a vital role not only as a medium of exchange, but also as a sophisticated tool for measuring economic value.

In this scenario, it functions as a unit of measurement that assigns tangible value to a wide range of goods and services, facilitating a concrete assessment of their relative importance. Consider the vastness and complexity of the modern economy, with its multiplicity of everyday transactions. Without a standardized unit of account, the valuation of goods and services would be an inextricable chaos. Here comes into play the crucial role of currency as a common reference, the reference point through which we assess and compare the value of goods and services.

Imagine walking through a market full of variety: fresh fruit, clothing, electronics, professional services and more. Each item or service has its own intrinsic value, but it is through currency that you can transform this diversity of values into a uniform. That price attached to each product is the result of an evaluation using currency as the unit of measure. This amount is what allows us to directly compare the value of a basket of apples with that of a new jacket or a legal counsel session.

However, it is not just a simple measure. The unit of account of currency is also fundamental to relative pricing.

Through confronting the prices of different goods and services, we can assess spending opportunities in terms of economic advantage.

This is how we make thoughtful decisions about the allocation of our financial resources, balancing our demand for items of different value.

In addition, currency as a unit of account plays a role in directing economic behavior. Companies set prices for their products by considering not only production costs, but also consumers' perception of value. Consumers, on the other hand, make decisions based on relative prices and the relationship between price and the utility they perceive from the product.

But the importance of money extends far beyond its immediate role as a medium of exchange. It serves a dual function that profoundly influences our relationship with financial resources. One of these functions is the ability to defer over time the portion of income that we do not immediately require to meet our consumption needs. In more accessible terms, it allows us to save a slice of current income to spend later.

Imagine owning a sur-plus amount of money than what you intend to use now. This sur-plus could be seen as a momentary surplus of wealth, but money makes it possible to save this surplus for a future time when it may be more needed or appropriate. This ability to save opens the door to a broader concept of financial management, in which not only immediate needs are considered, but also future possibilities and needs. This ability to conserve money not only enables the accumulation of resources, but also plays a key role in activating long-term in-investment.

People have been able to approach time- and resource-intensive grandiose pro-jects by being able to set aside a portion of their current income and preserve it for the future. This could be acquiring a house, starting a business, or investing in education. The very idea of "saving" thus acquires greater depth, as it is not only about accumulating money, but also about investing that money to seize opportunities beyond the immediate present.

## Evolution of money

The appearance of money can be traced back to very ancient times and represents a milestone in the evolution of human society. The earliest examples can be traced to Sumerian and Babylonian civilizations, in the period from about 3000 B.C. to 2000 B.C.

Objects such as shells, gold nuggets or animal skins were used as a medium of exchange to simplify trade transactions, which until then had been based on barter. These objects had an intrinsic value and were accepted by all as a form of payment for goods and services. However, the use of tangible goods as currency of exchange presented operative problems and was often inconvenient. Later, as civilizations developed, humans devised a new form of payment represented by discs of precious metal: coins. These standardized values facilitated exchange and represented a universally recognized and accepted commodity.

The success of this new form of payment brought an exponential increase in trade and in volumes of coins passed from hand to hand, eventually highlighting the main limitation of coins: their weight.

An even more efficient method of exchange was introduced by paper coins, which emerged during the Chinese Tang dynasty (618-907 AD). Easy to transport and use, these paper currencies made rapid and smooth trans-actions possible, contributing significantly to the development of trade and facilitating the expansion of economic at- activities, thus enabling the accumulation of considerable wealth.

Cash, the oldest and most tangible form of money, is still widely used today. They represent the physical manifestation of monetary value and offer a feeling of tangibility in transactions. The use of cash is intrinsically linked to privacy, as cash transactions leave no digital traces.

However, with the advent of new technologies, the use of cash is decreasing in favour of more convenient and efficient solutions. These different forms of money go beyond the traditional image of coins and banknotes, opening up new horizons in everyday transactions and financial interaction.

Credit cards have introduced a revolution in payment methods. Due to their lightness and practicality in carrying, they enable instant transactions both in physical stores and online. In addition, they offer some flexibility in purchasing, allowing you to pay later, thus providing temporary relief from the need to report cash. However, it is critical to properly manage transactions to avoid the deceptive pitfall of deferred financing with high interest rates and excessive debt accumulation. If you do not pay regularly and in full, the high interest rates applied to your remaining balances can accumulate debt quickly, trans-forming a seemingly small purchase into a substantial summa to repay.

To avoid this situation, it is essential to create a realistic budget, plan purchases carefully, and make full payments each month.

Electronic money, or e-money, is a digital manifestation of monetary value. This type of money includes not only debit cards, but also mobile apps and online payment platforms. It offers a fast and contactless payment experience, often linked to a specific bank account or app. E-money is particularly well suited for online transactions and digital commerce due to its convenience and security.

Cryptocurrencies represent a more re-centered frontier of money. The first digital currencies appeared in the 1980s, but the real turning point for the advent of cryptocurrencies came in 2009 with the creation of Bitcoin, the world's first and most popular cryptocurrency.

Virtual currencies and online payment systems have transformed the way money flows in the world. Money is no longer just a coin or a banknote; it has become virtual, intangible, and quickly moveable from place to place with the click of a button. But while they have further simplified transactions, they have raised new challenges regarding security and the management of personal finances. Coins such as Bitcoin and Ethereum have revolutionized the concept of currency, offering a form of digital money that is not tied to government entities or traditional financial institutions. While cryptocurrencies offer security and anonymity, they are also subject to volatility and regulatory uncertainty.

Finally, virtual money is a form of money utilized in contexts of online games or virtual worlds. Although it has no value in the real world, it can be exchanged within specific digital environments for virtual goods or services. This form of money highlights the intersection of the digital and financial worlds.

This intricate financial reality has introduced a new kind of challenge in which failure to learn the dynamics can have serious consequences. Knowledge of these various modes of money is crucial to successfully navigating the modern financial world and meeting the challenges and exploiting the opportunities presented by new technologies.

In this journey through the various forms of money that have shaped human history, we discovered how deep and diverse the concept of value is. From ancient forms of barter to modern financial instruments, money has spanned centuries and cultures, always remaining at the center of our economic activities. Under its many facets, money reflects our social evolution and is a witness to the technological advances that have made the contemporary financial world possible. Regardless of the form it takes, money is a catalyst for exchange, a resource to be managed wisely, and a reflection of our aspirations and the challenges we face.

And as we continue to push the boundaries of the financial future, let us remember that money is not just a medium of exchange, but a thread that binds the stories and lives of countless individuals through time.

## Limited resources and financial choices

Money is a precious and limited resource. This limitation is reflected both at the level of entire countries, where central banks must carefully regulate the issuance of money to ensure a balance with economic activity, and at the individual level as each person has limited income and savings at his or her disposal.

On the other hand, we have needs and desires that are il-limited because of the complex and changing nature of human aspiration. The desire for self-improvement, technological innovation, and continuous social progress push people to constantly seek new ways to meet their needs and achieve their goals. This discrepancy between our financial resources and our needs creates a situation in which we must make decisions about priorities and how to allocate our money.

Financial choices are therefore about balancing our limited resources with our goals and desires. It is about deciding what is most important and how we want to allocate our resources to meet those priorities. For example, you may want to save for the purchase of a house, but at the same time you would like to treat yourself to a vacation. Unless you have sufficient financial resources, you cannot do both at the same time.

Therefore, you will have to make a choice between these two options and decide which one is more important to you at that time in your life.

In addition, the finite nature of money also requires us to make choices about our long-term financial management. We must think about the future and consider how to invest our money so that it grows over time and provides us with greater financial security.

These financial choices can be complex and require balancing present and future needs without com-promising too much of our current well-being.

## Money-related emotions and perceptions

As we have seen, money plays a fundamental role in our daily lives, evoking a wide range of emotions and perceptions. Exploring these emotional nuances and their impact on our relationship with money is a crucial step in making informed financial decisions.

Among the emotions that money arouses, the sense of security is preeminent. Having the essential resources to meet basic needs and deal with unexpected situations generates a sense of security. This aspiration for protection motivates saving and long-term planning, creating a financial safety net to be used in case of need.

But money has the power to trigger anxiety and pre-occupation. The fear of not having enough money, losing a job, or facing unexpected expenses can trigger stress. Conscious money management is a process that goes beyond simply analyzing numbers. It requires attense attention to the emotions and perceptions surrounding our financial choices. Finding a balance between the rational and emotional aspects becomes crucial to making wise and informed financial decisions. Often, emotions influence our choices significantly. Anxiety may cause us to avoid risks that could instead prove beneficial, while ambition may push us to take impulsive actions. Awareness of these emotions allows us to take them into consideration without being dominated by them.

Finding a balance between emotions and reason helps us develop a more comprehensive approach to financial management. It enables us to make informed decisions, carefully weighing the practical aspects as well as the emotional implications. In this way, we can build a sound financial foundation that reflects our goals, priorities, and overall well-being.

It is important to remember that success is not exclusively determined by money. Our well-being derives from a variety of factors, including relationships, health, and cultivating personal passions. Finding a balance between a commitment to financial success and caring for life's deeper values is essential to achieving authentic realization.

## Money and personal goals

Money, a most powerful tool, assumes the role of moto-re propeller for a wide range of personal goals and life aspirations. Its possibilities embrace a wide range: first, it can meet basic needs such as housing, nourishment and education, the foundations of which are indispensable for leading a dignified life.

Beyond basic needs, money is an ally in the materialization of dreams and passions. If your soul is anchored in the desire to travel, you can employ the resource to explore new cultures and lands. If, on the other hand, your inclination turns to the creative sphere, you can invest in courses or equipment to enhance your artistic skills.

But its potential does not end there: it can act as a guarantor of your financial stability over time. By investing in an emergency fund or a retirement plan, you can ensure a peaceful old age and face unforeseen events with peace of mind.

In addition, money can be a vehicle for solidarity, a means of supporting causes that nourish your heart. The act of philanthropy represents a powerful way to positively influence the lives of others and contribute to the creation of a better society.

Nevertheless, do not fall into the illusion that the amount of money you possess is the only indicator of success or happiness. It is essential to balance financial ambitions with other fundamental aspects of your life such as relationships, health, and mental well-being.

## Money's role in social structure

The question of how wealth and morality intertwine and influence each other has challenged the human mind for centuries, stimulating debate and reflection in every corner of the world. In the vast backdrop of the human condition, the connection between material abundance and ethical values appears as a tangled web, woven by cultural, historical, and personal influences.

Although it may seem like an insoluble puzzle, the exploration of this complex connection can offer a fascinating and multifaceted picture of human nature and society. First, it is important to recognize that wealth and morality are two distinct but closely interconnected dimensions of human existence.

Wealth, understood as an abundance of material and financial resources, can influence an individual's choices and actions. On the other hand, morality refers to the principles and values that guide a person's ethical behavior. The challenge arises when these two dimensions come into conflict, pushing the individual to balance the pursuit of financial well-being with a moral code that transcends the accumulation of wealth.

In a broader perspective, the relationship between wealth and morality can be analyzed through different cultural lenses. In some societies, wealth is seen as a symbol of success and personal fulfillment, while in al-three it may be associated with a lack of moral integrity.

These perspectives are often rooted in a culture's history and tradition and can profoundly influence how individuals evaluate their wealth and behavior.

Morality can also influence the pursuit and use of wealth. Some may see wealth as a resource to be used to promote the common good, while others may focus on selfish accumulation. This raises important ethical questions: is it morally right to seek personal wealth at the expense of others? Should the pursuit of profit be guided by ethical limits? These are dilemmas that have fueled philosophical and ideological debates for centuries.

A crucial aspect of the complex relationship between wealth and morality is the role of power and social inequalities. The unequal distribution of wealth can generate social tensions and influence perceptions of morality. When some people accumulate immense fortune while others struggle to meet basic needs, questions about justice and fairness arise. This can fuel a sense of injustice and trigger moral reactions that challenge dominant paradigms.

It is also important to consider that the concept of wealth is not limited to financial resources. Wealth can also manifest itself in the form of knowledge, opportunities, and social relations. In this sense, wealth can be a powerful tool for positive change and the promotion of morality. Individuals and organizations can use their wealth, independently of its form, to address social and ethical issues, contributing to a more equitable and inclusive society.

Addressing the complexities of the connection between wealth and morality requires deep reflection and critical e-scrutiny of personal values. Everyone is called to confront his or her financial choices and their impact on his or her life and society as a whole complex. Wealth can provide opportunities to promote goodness and justice, but it can also be morally challenging when it conflicts with ethical values.

Often, society teaches us to create a negative image of people who have achieved a certain amount of wealth, associating them with selfish and unethical behavior. This limiting belief may have deep roots and be influenced by various sources, such as family, friends, or the media.

However, we must challenge this prejudice and understand that money is not the determining factor in defining a person's goodness or badness. Being rich does not automatically make someone a bad person, just as being poor does not automatically make someone a good person. The truth is that money is only a tool; it can offer you opportunities and comfort, but it cannot change who you are inwardly. If you are a generous person, having more financial resources will only be able to amplify your generosity and enable you to help others in more meaningful ways. On the other hand, if you are a stingy and selfish person, having more money will not change your nature. You define your personality and values, not money. What really matters is how a person decides to use his money and how he acts in society.

Therefore, do not let biases and limiting beliefs stand in your way of achieving the financial success you desire. Be aware of your values and the goals you wish to achieve in life. Learning to manage money responsibly and wisely, using it as a tool to achieve one's goals and to do good for one's community.

Always remember that your true character and your commitment to doing good in the world will be the true indicators of your goodness, regardless of your financial wealth. Money is like a magic wand that offers us the opportunity to explore new worlds and realize our dreams. With money we can buy our favorite toys, travel to distant shores, or help others. It is truly wonderful to have the power to do all these things, but it is important to realize that money can have a double face.

# Chapter 2

# Money generation

Money production is a vital component of the economy. Governments and financial institutions, such as central banks, are responsible for issuing national currency, whether in the form of coins or paper banknotes. These authorities regulate the amount of money in circulation and set its value, following economic and political criteria. But how does money get into people's pockets?

Imagine money as a traveler. As we ably examined, the journey begins at the central bank. Once created, money starts its journey to commercial banks, where we, as individuals, open our accounts. When we deposit our savings in these banks, we are entrusting them with the money. Commercial banks take a portion of these funds and lend them to other people or businesses that need them. That is the way they share money with the community. Those who receive loans will use the funds for purposes such as buying a house, starting a business, or financing college studies. Thus, the money continues its journey. People and businesses that receive these loans will spend the funds to purchase products and services. When we spend these funds, we transfer them to other per- sons or businesses, creating a continuous cycle. It is fundamental to emphasize that earning money must be done through lawful and moral activities.

The creation of counterfeit cash or the use of deceptive methods to earn profits are outlawed and can lead to serious legal consequences. To accumulate money in a righteous and responsible manner, it is vital to invest in one's skills and training, seek job opportunities, start sustainable businesses, and spend a portion of earned income.

Facing the daunting challenge of generating wealth is one of the most challenging tasks for young people today. However, addressing this challenge effectively requires a philosophical approach. Indeed, the process of creating de-gain goes beyond the mere accumulation of material goods. It is an experience that takes us deep inside ourselves, a journey that requires self-discipline and deep self-realization. Modern society teaches us that money is a tool for obtaining material goods and satisfying desires. But money creation can also be seen as the art of creating value, contributing to the community, and realizing our potential. Value creation is a multidimensional process, and often the value created goes far beyond the pure monetary aspect.

An entrepreneur who starts an innovative company, for example, may create value by providing products or services that meet people's needs or solve specific problems in society. But in addition to generating profits for himself and his shareholders, he provides jobs that stimulate economic growth and contribute to social progress. Similarly, an artist who creates works of art contributes by offering inspiration, reflection, and entertainment. These artistic expressions can be valuable to society, shaping culture, arousing emotions, and stimulating critical thinking. In this way, money becomes tangible recognition of the value we offer to the community through our capacities and engagement.

In any case, it is crucial to strike a balance between the aspiration to generate profit and the mission to create value. It is easy to fall into the trap of making money the central goal, which can lead to selfish or socially damaging behavior. On the other hand, focusing exclusively on value creation can have negative consequences on the economic sustainability of the enterprise and, consequently, on its very existence. Finding the right balance between these two objectives is crucial for responsible and successful business management.

It is necessary, therefore, to adopt a broader perspective, where value creation is the core of our action, and money one of the natural consequences of that commitment. By embracing this perspective, we can strive to per-sue financial goals without losing sight of the deeper meaning to of our action; we use money as a tool to realize our potential and to la-surely make a positive imprint on society, for it is in this way that we can truly derive satisfaction and meaning from our lives.

The journey to money-making begins with self-knowledge. Understanding our talents, passions and goals allows us to identify opportunities that align with our essence, without necessarily following predefined patterns for financial success, but seeking our own unique path. The key lies in combining our passions with the needs of the outside world.

Another crucial aspect in creating money is the ability to adapt to change. The way we handle money must be inherently flexible and open to change. An entrepreneurial attitude, which does not just create a company, but is ready to seize opportunities and innovate, becomes essential to prosper in a rapidly changing world.

You may be tempted to desire quick results and easy gains, but true financial success requires a holistic approach, cultivating virtues such as patience and moderation, which help you resist the temptations of unsustainable and often fallacious shortcuts.

## The money cycle

In the financial world, the concept of the "Money Cycle" represents an essential sequence of interconnected stages: earning, saving and investing. This cycle reflects the vital flow of our financial resources and guides us through the path to intelligently manage the money we earn.

Each stage plays a crucial role in shaping our financial future, enabling us to build a solid foundation and achieve our desired goals. Good income allows us to save more and invest better. Good saving helps reduce financial risk and achieve our financial goals. Good investing allows assets to grow over time. The Money Cycle describes the different stages through which money enters our lives, is used and grows. It is a continuous process that repeats itself over times.

The first phase of the Cycle is the "Gain." This is the stage when we receive income, whether it is represented by compensation for a job done, a cash gift, or simple weekly pocket money for younger people. Learning how to earn money from the earliest stages of productive life is a valuable lesson in financial responsibility. This experience teaches us the importance of evaluating our financial actions and decisions wisely and consciously. When we earn money, we become more careful about our spending and learn to distinguish between needs and wants.

Awareness of the value of money motivates us to save for future goals, such as college or trips, and gives us the opportunity to gradually build a stable financial base. Seeing income as an opportunity for financial growth inspires us to invest wisely and plan for a financially secure future. Responsible money management gives us the foundation to make informed financial decisions that will stay with us throughout our lives.

The second stage of the Cycle is "Saving." After earning the money, we must decide what to do with it. It is essential to resist the temptation of instant gratification and take a responsible approach to spending. Going out often to eat out, subscribing to underused online services, or giving in to the lure of a new fashionable cell phone are financial choices that can seriously damage our financial well-being. Conversely, setting aside even a small portion of earnings helps us build a solid financial foundation, enabling us to meet unexpected expenses or goal future goals, such as travel or buying a car.

The third stage is "Investing." Once we have saved enough, we can consider using our money to purchase in-investments that will allow us to grow our re-spending over time.

The Money Cycle is a continuous process that repeats itself over time. Each time we earn, save, and invest, the Money Cycle begins again. By going through the Cycle, you can accumulate financial resources, build an emergency fund, plan for retirement, and accomplish goals such as buying a house or a car.

Wise management of the Money Cycle requires planning, financial discipline and awareness of investment opportunities. Monitoring one's budget, avoiding debt, and adopting appropriate investment strategies are key elements in getting the most value from this financial cycle.

## The first opportunity to learn and grow

The most common step toward generating money is to enter the world of work. This can be done through part-time jobs, internships or full-time employment. Entering the world of work represents an experience that mixes emotions of excitement and fear, as it is a time dense with challenges. It is at this instant that you are faced with a series of crucial decisions that will go on to affect your future and your professional career.

Initially, it is critical to focus on jobs that provide experience and opportunities for professional growth, even though they may not be as rewarding as others but offer limited prospects for advancement. It is understandable that you wish to earn enough to live comfortably and perhaps afford some of life's little joys. However, I want to make you think about an equally important aspect: the formation of your competencies and your growth as a professional.

Imagine taking a job that pays you very well, but where you perform repetitive tasks with no room for learning or personal development. In the first moment you might be satisfied with the amount on your pay check, but soon you might feel bored, dissatisfied, and unmotivated. Those days without a challenge and a chance to grow could begin to take a toll, both on your mental well-being and on your prospects.

On the other hand, imagine starting a job that may not pay much at first, but offers you a challenging environment and a wide range of skills to acquire. Here you will have the opportunity to put your knowledge into practice and learn new knowledge. You could be involved in exciting projects and work with experienced people who can become mentors for you.

Remember that your first job does not need to be your final one for life. It is an important stage in your career path, but it can also be an opportunity to explore and discover what you really are passionate about.

Choosing a job that fosters your growth and the development of your skills is an investment in your career. The skills you acquire will not only have value in your current career but may also prove to be keys to unforeseen opportunities in different fields. Your flexibility and ability to learn become increasingly relevant as you progress in your career path. Take the time to evaluate what you really want to get out of your career and how you can achieve those goals.

Then, be wise in your choice. Don't let the prospect of immediate gain distract you from the importance of investing in your professional growth and development. Think about your future and remember that the road to a satisfying career is often made up of cordial and forward-looking choices. The satisfaction and sense of achievement that will result from learning and professional creation will be key elements in your long-term success. Over time, solid experience and a well-developed skill set will translate into higher remuneration.

Professional growth and related remuneration have an important counterbalance represented by one's personal life. The image of the exhausted worker, caught between endless hours in the office and the obligation to respond to the constant demands of the digital age, is slowly la-singing space to new work paradigms and a renewed appreciation of personal well-being. With the evolution of working arrangements, such as teleworking and flextime, the possibility of reconciling professional and personal needs has become a reality, allowing for a reduction in stressful commuting and favoring the optimal distribution of time between the various spheres of life.

It will therefore be worthwhile to evaluate the policies adopted by the company when choosing one's employment to check the congruity of these with one's specific needs, keeping in mind, however, that one's individual responsibility plays a crucial role. Learning the art of defining clear boundaries between work responsibilities and time for rest is crucial to maintaining optimal mental and physical well-being. Due to the increasing presence of technology, the line between work and personal life is often blurred, creating tensions that negatively affect both psychological and economic wellbeing. In this context, appropriate management of one's time plays a vital role.

Acquiring strategies for organizing activities efficiently, identifying priorities, and knowing how to identify moments of necessary rest can help prevent situations of stress and overload. Finding the balance between time off and work engagement proves to be an effective way to ensure consistent productivity in the long run.

The work environment is also a consideration when choosing one's employment since these influences not only professional performance but also the overall well-being of employees. An inclusive corporate culture, positive dynamics among colleagues and a constructive relationship with superiors contribute to the creation of a stimulating and rewarding work environment.

Corporate culture and values form the foundation of any organization. Companies that put ethical values, sustainability and respect for diversity into practice not only attract talent but promote a working environment where each individual feels valued and listened to. A culture based on transparency, collaboration, and empowerment promotes innovation and a sense of belonging.

The dynamics among colleagues play an alt-ret-right role. Effective collaboration, knowledge sharing, and mutual support are key factors for productivity and well-being. Companies that encourage the formation of cohesive teams and openness to dialogue contribute to creating a climate in which learning, and growth are encouraged. Relationships with superiors are also critically important in creating a healthy work environment. Empathetic and support-oriented leadership fosters open communication, in which employees feel free to express opinions and concerns. In addition, management that recognizes and values everyone's contribution stimulates a sense of accomplishment and motivation.

It is important to note that a positive working environment not only influences the psychological well-being of employees, but also has a tangible impact on productivity and company performance. Satisfied and motivated employees are more likely to devote energy and importance to work activities, thus improving the quality of service provided.

Another element of fundamental importance, not only for business efficiency, but especially for the well-being of employees, is safety in the workplace. Strict norms and company policies aimed at accident prevention are essential elements in creating a safe and healthy work environment, defining standards and procedures to prevent accidents and minimize risks to workers' health. These standards cover several aspects, including the proper handling of hazardous substances, the use of personal protective equipment and the organization of workspaces. Companies committed to workplace safety adopt prevention policies aimed at identifying and minimizing risks.

These policies may include training programs on safety procedures, evacuation simulations, and the promotion of informed behavior among employees. In addition, many companies invest in advanced security equipment and technologies that reduce the risks associated with certain tasks. Promoting employee health is an equally important aspect of corporate policies. Initiatives such as promoting healthy lifestyles, providing wellness programs, and creating ergonomic work environments help keep employees physically and mentally healthy. In this way, companies demonstrate a real commitment to the well-being of their employees, as well as to safety.

Too often, we are so focused on finding a job that provides a steady income that we overlook the latent potential that dwells within us. Each of us has unique passions and talents. These are our strengths, our most valuable assets. Often, however, we do not realize their potential. We just use them for our leisure time, without thinking about how they could help us build a more fulfilling and gratification life.

The world is thirsty for creativity and for personals willing to showcase their skills. There is invaluable value in knowing how to save and invest wisely, but there is just as much value in knowing how to capitalize on what makes us unique, and yes, your passions can become a source of income: what do you love to do most?

You can turn your passion for cooking, writing, drawing, or playing an instrument into a lucrative business no matter what your passion is. Your skill in communication, organization or problem-solving can be valuable to others and thus become a job opportunity.

If you want to discover your passions and skills with a view to producing value, here are some tips:

- Make a list of all the things you are passionate about. What do you like doing in your spare time? What are the things that make you feel happy and fulfilled?

- Think about your talents. What are you good at? What are the things you do best?

- Look for ways to combine your passions and talents. How can you use your passions to create something new and valuable?

- Don't be afraid to experiment. There is no right or wrong way to discover your passions and talents. The important thing is to start and never stop.

Exploring your passions and talents is an exciting journey. It is a journey that can lead you to discover new things about yourself and the world around you. It is a journey that can help you build a more fulfilling and rewarding life. The idea of following your passions and skills can have a positive impact on society. When people can work in a field they love and are passionate about, they are more motivated and productive. This can lead to increased efficiency and competitiveness in the economy. In addition, people who are satisfied with their work are more likely to be involved in the community and contribute to society.

Here are some examples of how you can turn your passions and skills into income:

-   Create a blog or website. If you have a passion for writing, you can create a blog or website where you can share your ideas and knowledge with others. You can also earn money through publicity, selling products or services, or sponsoring companies.

-   Become a freelancer. If you have specialized skills, you can offer your services as an independent professional. There are many websites where you can find clients, such as Up work, Fiverr and Freelancer.com.

-   Create your own business. If you have an entrepreneurial idea, you can create your own business. There are many ways to start a business, but it is important to do your research and have a clear plan.

No matter which path you choose, remember that the most important thing is to follow your passions and talents. If you do something you enjoy, you will be more motivated to work hard and achieve your goals.

## Value creation

One of the key concepts in accumulating wealth is the capacity of offering products or services that respond to the needs and desires of one's target audience-that group of individuals to whom a company targets with its offerings. When you can identify what people need or want and you are able to meet those demands, you create value and thus be recommitted for your business. This is the basis of entrepreneurship and financial success.

The first step in creating money is therefore, comprehending the market and identifying what people are looking for or wanting. During this crucial process, market research plays a crucial role in providing us with the information we need to make informed and strategic decisions. But how is market research accomplished?

I n a nutshell, it is a process of collecting and analyzing data regarding a particular market, which allows us to better understand its needs, desires, behaviors, and consumer preference. This information helps us individuate opportunities, assess the competition, and define our unique value proposition. The market research process can be divided into several stages:

1. **Identification of Objectives**: First, we need to clarify the objectives of our research. What do we want to discover? What information is crucial to our business or financial project? Defining the objectives allows us to focus on the most relevant information.

2. **Primary Data Collection**: Primary data collection consists of gathering information directly from consumers or the target market. This can be done through surveys, interviews, focus groups, or field observations. This data is specific to our target and gives us direct insight into the needs and behaviors of our potential customers.

3. **Secondary Data Collection**: Secondary data is information that is already available and collected from external sources, such as market studies, reports, articles, or statistics. These sources may provide demographic data, market trends, competitive in-formation, and more. Secondary data are often a valuable resource as they allow us to get a broad overview of the market quickly and inexpensively.

4. **Analysis and Interpretation of Data**: Once we have collected the da-ducts, it is essential to analyze and interpret them correctly. Analysis allows us to identify patterns, trends, and hidden opportunities. Interpreting data means translating in-formation into concrete strategies for our financial plan.

Among the wide range of information that research can provide us with, the most relevant include:

- Identifying our target audience: Co-knowing our audience allows us to tailor our offering to their specific needs.

- Competitor analysis: Studying our competitors helps us uniquely position ourselves and individuate competitive advantages.

- Assessment of market trends: Understanding trends enables us to anticipate changes and seize new opportunities.

- Price and profitability analysis: we can establish competitive and sustainable prices when we understand the prices charged in the market and the profitability of different options.

- Customer satisfaction assessment: Knowing the level of satisfaction of our customers helps us to improve our products or services and to co-build lasting relationships.

Once a need or desire has been identified, it is moment to develop a service or product that can respond to those requests.

The key to success in this crucial process is the value proposition. Your service or product must be more than just an object or idea; the goal is not just to create something that you think is great, but to create something that is meaningful to others, i.e. that can solve real problems for your customers. Place your focus on satisfying your audience. By offering something authentic and valuable, you will arouse people's enthusiasm and their willingness to pay for it, and financial success will be achieved-naturally. Be determined to focus on the quality of your offering and constantly keep a watchful eye on the needs of your audience.

Everything is changeable and life is constantly evolving. Continuous improvement is the key to staying abreast of changing market demands and ensuring that what you offer always lives up to expectations.

When you put yourself in the mindset of creating value for others, you will not only improve the lives of the people around you, but your financial situation will also benefit greatly from that mindset. Generosity and dedication to value creation result in a positive reputation, loyal customers, and long-term growth opportunities.

## One, two, ...many sources of income

At a time when economic uncertainty and market fluctuations are the order of the day, the ability to cultivate and manage diverse sources of income becomes a crucial step in ensuring long-term financial stability. Diversifying income sources not only provides greater protection against uncertainty, but also creates a solid base on which to build lasting economic security. Diversifying income not only mitigates risk, but also provides flexibility, adaptability, and a pathway to achieve ambitious financial goals.

Over the years, the financial world has noticeably changed. Global economies have become increasingly interconnected, and financial crises have demonstrated the importance of not depending on a single source of income. Financial stability has become an increasingly difficult goal to achieve, as unforeseen events can have a significant impact on personal finances. It is therefore essential to diversify income sources to minimize financial risks.

The concept of multiple sources of income ("Multiple Streams of Income") was introduced and made widely popular by Robert G. Allen, an American author and entrepreneur, through his book of the same name in which he provided concrete guidelines on how to implement this strategy.

Diversification of income sources can take place in several ways. One can consider diversifying la- work, for example, by seeking supplementary income opportunities such as freelancing or part-time work. At the same time, one can consider investing in passive income-generating activities or projects, such as renting property or returns from financial investments. In addition, you can consider starting an entrepreneurial business or developing a personal project that can generate additional income.

Here are some practical ideas on how to generate money and create sources of income:

- **Employment**: Work for an employer or company and earn a salary or wage.

- **Self-employment**. Offer services or expertise as a freelancer or consultant and charge fees to clients.

- **Affiliations and marketing**: Earning commission by promoting other people's products or services through affiliate programs or affiliate marketing.

- **Content creation**: Earn money by creating online content such as blogs, YouTube videos, podcasts, or writing books.

- **Selling physical goods**: Selling and buying physical goods, such as physical products or antiques, through physical or online stores.

- **Training and education**: Offering courses, workshops, webinars, or consulting on topics of competence.

- **Gig economy**: Doing freelance work or temporary work through online platforms, such as Uber, Airbnb, or freelance platforms

- **Passions and hobbies**: Make money from your passions or hobbies, such as selling crafts, artwork or collectibles.

- **Recycling and selling**: Collect and resell used or rare items, such as vintage, antiques or collectibles.

These are just a few examples of the different ways you can create money.

The key is to find approaches that fit your skills, interests and financial goals. The diverse sources of income approach can bring an additional valuable benefit: the ability to devote time and resources to one's personal passions and interests, thus contributing to greater individual satisfaction. Diversifying income sources also has the advantage of accelerating the achievement of financial goals. With more resources available, one can invest and save more. Diversified sources of income also offer greater financial risibility in case of emergencies or unforeseen situations. If one source of income is interrupted, others can provide a safety net. In addition, diversification promotes the development of diverse skills and fosters adaptability in unforeseen situations.

We have examined numerous benefits associated with di-versification of income sources. However, it is crucial to emphasize that implementing and managing multiple sources of income requires planning, discipline and scrupulous attention.

It is essential to accurately assess opportunities and risks while maintaining constant monitoring of the performance of each income source. In addition, it is fundamental to balance the time and resources devoted to each source of income to maximize total benefits while avoiding the risk of exhaustion.

## Generative Assets: how to create passive income

In the financial world, there is a concept that is gaining more and more relevance: passive income. This term represents an alternative route to traditional income from a salaried job. Imagine an economic opportunity that does not require an intentional time commitment on your part but, instead, works tirelessly on your behalf. The innate power of generative assets emerges here: real estate, stocks, and businesses.

These are not mere items on a list, but rather fascinating pillars of your financial autonomy, enabling you to reap the rewards as you continue your path.

Let's start with the example of real estate. Buying property to rent can be a great way to generate passive income streams. Once you find reliable tenants and establish a lease, you will receive monthly rents, which will be an ongoing income stream. In addition, over the years, property values tend to increase, allowing you to benefit from asset appreciation.

Stocks are another tool that can produce passive income on a constant basis. When you acquire shares in a company, you become the owner of a small part of that company. If the company distributes its profits to its shareholders through dividends, you receive a portion of those profits in the form of passive income. When you decide to sell the shares, you may also realize capital gains if their value increases over time.

Investing in businesses is a more complex option, but it can be extremely rewarding. Instead of starting your own business, you can invest in existing enterprises as a partner. If the business is successful, you will receive a portion of the profits as passive income.

The essence behind the potential of generative assets, as income tools, lies in giving them enough time. It is in this simple step that their financial magic is unleashed, allowing them to reach their maximum value. For example, if you are investing in real estate to rent it out, it may take time to find the right in-tenants or to benefit from property value appreciations.

Similarly, the financial environment is notorious for its volatility, and it may take a while for companies to distribute dividends or for stock values to show a significant increase. A long-term mindset, coupled with a good dose of patience and capacity to adapt to changing situations, will be fundamental to avoiding impulsive decisions based on short-term market fluctuations.

You may not see immediate results, but that does not mean the investment is not worthwhile. You will need to carefully monitor your investments, adjust when necessary, and trust in the long-term growth process. Establish a sound investment plan and stick to it over time. Avoid being influenced by current trends or ephemeral news. Instead, make thoughtful decisions based on your financial goals and risk appetite.

Once you've built a portfolio of assets that can generate passive income streams, you'll enjoy greater financial freedom and additional income to help you achieve your financial goals and improve your quality of life.

## Make an investment in yourself

The uncontainable rise of technological innovations and global changes requires an unprecedented ability to adapt. The knowledge you gain and the skills you develop not only set you apart, but act as a foundation on which to build your financial and professional strategies.

This perspective is not limited to the mere growth of a set of skills; rather, it requires continuous evolution. Developing skills should not be interpreted as a pure career move, but as a path of soul enrichment and skill enhancement. This includes improving your communication, sharpening your problem solving, and expanding your intuition.

An investment in education and skills can increase career and earning opportunities in the long term. Adopting a proactive approach to learning and self-development also allows one to remain relevant and competitive in an ever-changing world. This can ensure continuity of employment and the possibility of adapting to new opportunities, avoiding the risk of becoming obsolete in the labor market.

Investing in yourself is not only found in the professional sphere. It is a choice that permeates every aspect of life, allowing for lasting personal growth. Cultivating passions outside of work, learning new practical skills and improving the quality of daily life are all natural consequences of a careful investment in oneself. The returns on such an investment extend far beyond the financial aspect. Each newly developed skill confers a sense of confidence and self-esteem that is reflected in all challenges, enabling one to overcome them with determination.

Greater knowledge and competence often also translate into better control over one's finances, the ability to make informed financial decisions and effectively manage money. In summary, investing in yourself is a vehicle for creating a solid financial foundation, achieving professional and personal goals and making the most of the opportunities that life presents.

## Financial planning is crucial

Financial planning is the crucial foundation in generating income effectively, then providing the map, resources, and direction needed to create a successful path toward achieving your financial goals and realizing a sound financial future. It is a strategic framework that enables you to optimize your income, minimize risk, and seize financial opportunities.

To achieve your financial goals and generate income intelligently and consistently, accurate financial planning is essential. This process identifies potential sources of income and maps out the path to reach your goals. It helps you set money accumulation goals, such as saving for travel, investing in real estate, starting a business, or planning for retirement.

Goals become the compass that guides financial decisions. Once established, planning assesses the current financial situation and creates a real-state path. Income, expenses, investments, and savings are considered, figuring out how much to save and invest to get closer to desired goals. Second, financial planning optimizes available resources, allowing strategic al-location of money and ranking between in-investments and expenditures to reduce waste.

This disciplined approach maximizes the potential for income growth, achieving more meaningful results with fewer resources. In addition, financial planning provides valuable decision support. For example, it is necessary to choose how to allocate savings among different investment options, such as stocks, bonds, mutual funds, or real estate. Such planning determines which combination of investments is best suited to your goals and level of risk. Wise financial management also allows you to save more efficiently. Learning how to allocate a portion of your monthly income helps build an emergency fund, which is essential for dealing with unforeseen events such as job loss or urgent medical expenses. In addition, systematic saving paves the way for investment, an essential element in ensuring financial stability and increasing your wealth.

Financial planning is also a shield against financial risks. Anticipating possible obstacles and unforeseen events allows you to take preventive measures, protecting the accumulated income from unexpected losses. In addition, careful financial planning helps to manage money responsibly by establishing a budget, reducing unnecessary expenses, and avoiding impulsive financial decisions. Que-this maintains control of finances and prevents situations of excessive debt. In addition, prudent finance management develops a long-term financial mindset, resisting the temptations of immediate spending and gratification and focusing on long-term goals, such as buying a home, retirement planning or starting a business. Financial planning promotes a proactive approach to income generation. Through the identification of opportunities and the definition of investment strategies, it allows one to capitalize on favorable market conditions and anticipate future challenges, contributing to the growth of money over time and ensuring a more prosperous financial future.

A long-term financial plan is a flexible, non-static guide that adapts to life's changes, but it is essential to review it periodically and make appropriate adjustments, especially in the case of significant events such as a change of job, marriage or parenthood. One of the keys to a successful financial plan is its flexibility and ability to adapt to changes in your financial situation and personal goals. Life is constantly evolving, and your financial plan must be ready to keep up with the pace. Here are a few tips on how to regularly update your plan to stay abreast of changes:

1. Review periods: Schedule regular review periods for your financial plan, such as every six months or once a year. During these reviews, take time to analyze your current financial situation and assess progress toward your goals. Identify any changes in your situation, such as a pay raise, a new job, or an unexpected expense, and consider how those events might affect your plan.

2. Set new goals: Over time, your personal goals may change. You may decide you want to buy a bigger house, change careers, or take a sabbatical to travel. Be sure to update your financial plan to reflect these new goals and establish a strategy for achieving them.

3. Adjust your investment strategy: Market conditions can change over time, which may require you to revise your investment strategy. If the market was going through a period of volatility, you might consider adopting a more conservative strategy. Conversely, if you are young and

have a long investment outlook, you might want to consider more aggressive investments.

4. Maintain a contingency fund: An emergency fund is a fundamental part of your financial plan and should be evaluated and updated regularly. Make sure you have enough financial resources to meet unforeseen expenses or emergency situations without putting a dent in your long-term investments.

5. Consult a financial advisor: If you feel overwhelmed by managing your financial plan or need specialized advice, do not hesitate to consult with a professional. An experienced financial advisor can help you assess your financial situation, identify opportunities and risks, and develop a strategy tailored to your goals.

6. Maintain discipline: Although your financial plan may require regular updates, it is important to maintain discipline and follow the established path. Avoid impulsive decisions based on short-term market fluctuations and always remember your long-term goals.

Always remember that every small step counts. Although it may seem that your initial capital is not enough, don't let that stop you. Start with what you have and over time, you will see your money grow through your efforts.

Chapter 3

# How to spend money

You have just entered the working world. I congratulate you; it is an exciting milestone, a step toward independence. From now on, every month you will be able to enjoy the fruits of your labor directly in your pocket. Finally, a real cakewalk after so many years of sacrifice and giving up those purchases you have longed for. Now is the time to enjoy the fruits of your hard work by indulging in what you have always wanted. The future is luminous and full of opportunities, and the money you have earned will be the means to realize your dreams. There is no longer any bi- need to delay or deprive yourself of small joys: you have deserved this moment, and it is time to enjoy it to the fullest...or is it?!

If, for a moment, you leave the euphoria aside, you may be able to sense it. It is a faint sound echoing in the distance, resonating in a corner of your consciousness. Almost a whisper, but you know you must pay attention to it. It is the bell of your future, and it is there to call you back to reality. If you let yourself be overcome by the impulse to spend every cent of your newly earned salary without limit, you risk undoing all the sacrifices and renunciations you have made over the past years. All that could vanish in a blink of an eye, leaving you without support when you need it most

But you need not fear: a solution exists and has already made its acquaintance in the previous chapter: financial planning. It is she who will provide you with the tools and strategies you need to avoid falling into the abyss of reckless spending. Through financial planning, you will learn to master money instead of being crushed by it. It is the key to taking control of your financial life, a weapon against the uncertainty that the future may bring.

Financial planning is not just a choice; it is a necessity if you want to build a secure foundation for yourself. Learning to spend wisely the money you earn can make the difference between stable financial serenity and continued financial anxiety. Administering your finances may seem complicated, but with a well-defined approach and a clear understanding of your financial priorities, you will be able to meet this challenge with confidence. With my help you will learn how to create a realistic budget, save for the unexpected, responsibly manage debt, and invest in your personal development so that you can build a solid financial foundation and successfully achieve your goals.

## Financial Priorities

When it comes to money management, it is critical to comprehend financial priorities, especially for young professionals like you who are just beginning their business careers. This means identifying financial goals, both short- and long-term, and establishing a clear vision for the future to guide personal finance management. To help you in this process you will find below a list of possible goals from which to identify your goals based on your aspirations and starting financial situation:

Short-Term Financial Goals:

1. Create an Emergency Fund: Accumulate an emergency fund equivalent to three to six months of expenses to deal with unforeseen situations such as medical expenses or job loss.

2. Getting rid of Debts: Pay off any high-interest debts, such as credit cards or personal loans, to free yourself from the burden of interest and improve your credit score.

3. Saving for a Vacation: Set aside money for a short vacation or weekend getaway, rewarding yourself with a time of relaxation and recreation.

4. Purchase a New Technology: Save for the purchase of a new technology device, such as a computer or smartphone, to improve productivity and connectivity.

5. Financial Insulation: Save to rent or ac-purchase a residence to become independent and provide housing stability.

Long-Term Financial Goals:

1. Retirement Fund: Begin contributing to a pension plan or individual retirement fund to ensure a financially secure future in old age.

2. Home Purchase: Saving for the purchase of a first home by investing in real estate and becoming rooted in the community.

3. Advanced Education: Investing in further study or training to improve career prospects and increase earning potential in the long run.

4. Investments: Begin investing in stocks, bonds or mutual funds to grow assets over time.

5. Starting a Business: Saving to start an entrepreneurial business, realizing the dream of being your own **boss** and earning independently.

6. Travel Around the World: Saving for an extended trip to explore different cultures and exotic places, creating lasting memories.

7. Donations and Charity: Create a fund for donations and charitable works, contributing to the community and helping those who are less fortunate.

8. Car Purchase: Save money to purchase a new or used car, improving mobility and convenience.

9. Marriage and Family: Prepare financially for marriage and future family by planning for expenses related to marriage, home and children.

10. Financial Freedom: Working toward the goal of achieving a situation where you have enough financial resources to choose how to spend your time without worrying about money.

Every individual has different financial priorities, and these can be influenced by personal values and unique life situations. It is essential to resist external pressures, the culture of consumerism or the desire to follow the crowd and focus on what is truly meaningful for one's financial future.

## Creating the budget

Now that you have identified your financial goals, it is time to shape your budget. Many young people see it as something unnecessary if not restricting, a list of prohibitions that muzzles their desires, a barrier between them and their passions.

It is not about caging your spending aspirations but rather guiding them toward the realization of your dreams, without getting lost along the way.

A well-structured budget is a key tool for understanding how money is spent, identifying areas where savings can be made, and planning for future goals. A budget provides financial freedom and control over your finances, allowing you to make informed financial decisions.

The cornerstone of creating an accurate budget is collecting financial data. Carefully, list all your monthly income, including not only your salary but also any other extra income; next, consider all your fixed and variable expenses, broken down into specific categories such as rent, bills, food and leisure.

This will give you a detailed overview of your spending habits and ease in planning for the future. Set realistic limits for each spending category to avoid overspending and stay aligned with your financial goals. Keep track of your spending periodically, using tools such as spreadsheets or dedicated apps to monitor each financial movement. By doing so, you will always have a true view of your economic situation and you will not run the risk of having an unusable tool in your hands because it is far from factual reality. Be honest with yourself and do not give in to the temptation to overestimate your expected income and try to be as accurate as possible in estimating future expenses.

Once you have reached this point, proceed by subtracting your total expenses from your monthly income. This will give you the monthly balance, which represents the difference between the amount you earn and the amount you spend during a specific period, usually a month. If the result is positive, it means that you are living below your possibilities, and this is a good sign. You can allocate some of the income to saving or investing for the future. If the balance is negative, you will have to make some adjustments to reduce expenses or increase income.

Responsible financial management will help you reach your goals, but don't forget to take care of yourself and allow yourself moments of joy along the way. It may be paradoxical, but reserving a percentage of one's budget to enjoy moments of leisure and fun conceals a profound wisdom. Leisure and fun are an integral part of your life. After all, work can be stressful and demanding, and setting aside time to relax and have fun is essential to your mental and emotional well-being.

When you include a portion for leisure in your budget, you are giving yourself a chance to enjoy life and have enjoyable experiences. You can go out with friends, try new hobbies or indulge in some small pleasure without feeling guilty. These moments of joy and contentment con-tribute to maintaining a balance in your life and help you stay motivated and satisfied.

Too much work and stress can lead you to feel exhausted and unmotivated. Taking time to relax and have fun will help you recharge your energy and be more productive at work.

Don't think that including a part for leisure in your budget means sacrificing your financial goals. You can strike a balance between saving and having fun so that you can live life to the fullest without compromising your financial future. Be conscious of your money, but also allow yourself to live in the present and enjoy life

With budgeting as your compass and control over your resources, you can navigate toward a prosperous and fulfilling financial future but remember to always keep your budget in check and update it regularly. Monitor your expenses and always strive to improve your financial situation.

## Track expenses

The idea of money as a constant stream, flowing through our hands like a river, prompts us to consider how we manage our financial resources. All too often, money slips away without our realizing it, driven by the temptations of impulsive buying or the apparent convenience of everyday expenses. And it is precisely in these moments that we understand the vital importance of keeping track of expenses.

Tracking expenses goes far beyond a simple registration of numbers on a sheet of paper. It is a way of increasing financial awareness, allowing us to shed light on how we really use our earnings. Although it may seem tedious at first, this act of monitoring is the key to more sound and conscious financial management.

Consider those small expenses we often take for granted: a quick cup of coffee, an entertainment app, a take-out snack. They seem harmless, but over time, they can add up in surprising ways. Keeping track of every transaction, no matter how small, helps us shed light on the shadow of these minimal expenses, revealing how much they can weigh on the overall budget.

Tracking expenses also has the power to lower the hectic pace of financial decisions. It forces us to pause and reflect: does it make sense to buy this item? Does this expenditure align with my long-term financial goals? This process of reflection generates a new form of gratification, one that comes from making thoughtful choices that promote our financial well-being.

Through this practice, we build a personal map of our finances, a sort of compass that guides our decisions toward greater financial stability. In the long run, it allows us to plan confidently for future goals, such as a trip or a significant investment. It also helps us distinguish between a real deal and a momentary temptation, making us less susceptible to impulsive purchases.

Today, technology makes it much easier to monitor spending through specially created apps and software. These tools not only simplify the recording of transactions, but also give us charts and analysis that reveal trends and habits. Moreover, expense tracking should be seen as an investment in our financial well-being, rather than a restriction

Tracking expenses acts as a kind of mirror that reflects our relationship with money. It is an act of financial self-awareness that can transform our financial perspective and behavior. From a simple control tool to a source of confidence in facing financial challenges, expense tracking gives us a unique perspective on the art of managing money wisely and responsibly.

By incorporating this practice into your life, you will build a solid foundation for managing your money wisely, ensure that every expense is a step towards your long-term financial well-being.

## Review and adapt

A budget represents a dynamic and living document. In a world that changes incessantly, a static budget amounts to an old, faded photograph. It is crucial to allow the budget to evolve and grow with us: through the recording of expenditures made, it continually adapts to the changing context of our existence.

Keeping one's budget up-to-date and fresh situates us in command of the financial future, making us able to face any unforeseen contingency with serenity and confidence. Therefore, we should never be afraid to look at the budget with different eyes, with an open mind and willing to change.

Undoubtedly, the first step is to outline an initial budget, however, the real importance lies in relentless iteration. Monitoring and reviewing one's budget should not be interpreted as a sign of weakness or difficulty; on the contrary, it testifies to financial wisdom and awareness. Reviewing allows it to be adapted to changing life, taking into account new priorities, ambitions and circumstances.

Each budget review can be used as an opportunity for financial introspection. Asking yourself some questions is crucial: what are your current goals? Which expenses are recurring and which could be reduced or totally eliminated? How can re-spending be optimized? Periodic budget reanalysis ensures the firm control of one's finances, preventing them from becoming a source of worry and stress.

Yet, this is not all. With each personal budget adjustment, one consciously takes control of one's financial narrative. In this way, one moves from being mere passive observers of one's economic trans-actions to becoming conscious authors of one's own monetary success story. Through such a review process, one gains the ability to adapt to the unforeseen challenges and opportunities that life holds, transforming each budget update into a step toward financial empowerment.

The personal budget represents a powerful and fundamental tool: by letting it grow and evolve with us, it will enable us to overcome limitations

## Planning for the necessary expenses

All those essential and unavoidable expenses that people face in their daily lives should be considered necessary. These expenses, although often overlooked, have significant power when it comes to shaping one's financial path. Understanding them and managing them effectively is critical to achieving financial stability and long-term success.

You might ask: Why should I bother planning for necessary expenses when they are unavoidable? The answer lies in the difference between reacting and planning proactively. By tracking necessary expenditures in advance, you can allocate your financial resources more efficiently, ensuring that you are adequately prepared to meet your obligations, whether it's paying bills, covering essential living expenses, or saving for future goals.

This proactive approach gives you a clear picture of your financial obligations. By identifying and quantifying essential expenses, such as rent or mortgage, utilities, groceries, transportation, insurance, and health care, you can better understand the destination of your money and make informed decisions accordingly. This knowledge can then serve as a basis for creating a realistic budget that aligns with your income and priorities, helping you achieve your financial goals, such as saving for retirement or making a down payment on a home.

In addition, planning for necessary expenses allows you to anticipate possible cash flow issues and prepare for due time. Often unforeseen events can occur, such as medical emergencies or breakdown repairs. By actively considering these possibilities and establishing an emergency fund, you can protect yourself against the unexpected and avoid accumulating debt or depleting your savings. This proactive approach is critical to maintaining financial security and providing peace of mind in moments of uncertainty.

To better understand the importance of planning for necessary expenses, let's consider a practical example. Here is Sarah, a young professional with ambitious career goals and a desire to achieve financial freedom. Analyzing her income and expenses, Sarah identifies that her necessary expenses include rent, utilities, transportation, groceries, and loan repayment. By planning these expenses in advance, Sarah determines the exact amount she needs to allocate to each category and puts it into her monthly budget. This meticulous planning not only allows Sarah to live within her means, but also allows her to save for her dream vacations and contribute to her retirement fund.

With a clear roadmap for her finances, Sarah has reduced financial stress and is confidently navigating her financial journey.

Thus, we have seen that planning for necessary expenses is an indispensable aspect of personal finance. By proactively planning and allocating financial re-sources for unavoidable expenses, you can gain better control over your financial life, achieve your goals, and secure your future.

Through meticulous planning, people can get a clear picture of their financial obligations, anticipate unforeseen events, and protect themselves. Careful planning of essential expenses lays the foundation for a more secure and prosperous future.

## Managing unforeseen expenses

Avoiding impulsive decisions and keeping calm in situations of unforeseen expenses are fundamental behaviors that require thoughtful consideration and a rational approach. In this regard, analysis of the magnitude of the unforeseen expense assumes a crucial role.

In case it is a minor expense, it is possible to opt for the redistribution of financial resources to cover this contingency. This approach may imply the reduction of nonessential consumption or the active search for alternative solutions. However, if the amount is considerable, it may be necessary to adopt more articulated strategies, such as selling assets or increasing revenues.

In order to avoid being unprepared for the eventuality, it is advantageous to establish guidelines to follow in order to deal optimally with unforeseen expenses. First, reviewing one's budget proves indispensable. This exercise makes it possible to make an accurate assessment of income and expenditure, thus identifying the resources available to cope with unforeseen events. In addition, it is advisable to carefully review planned expenses to assess the possibility of reducing some of them. This could include adopting attitudes such as preparing meals at home, limiting travel or eliminating unused subscriptions.

If the anticipated reduction in expenses does not cover unforeseen speciation, a right of first refusal may be considered. In this case, it is important to carefully compare the various options available and clearly understand the terms of the contract.

If, on the other hand, one opts to sell assets, it is essential to acquire in-depth knowledge of market prices in order to accurately assess this opportunity. Finally, when no immediate solution can be found to cover the unexpected expense, the option of deferring payment or seeking a vantage agreement with the creditor may be viable solutions.

In any case, it is advisable to act early to shelter yourself from these kinds of pitfalls by providing for a special item in your monthly budget.

This creates a financial cushion to meet unexpected expenses without touching your already accumulated savings or resorting to debt. It is important to determine the appropriate amount for this emergency fund, considering your monthly income and individual needs. You can choose to allocate a percentage of income or a fixed amount, depending on your financial situation. For example, you could start with the goal of allocating at least 5 percent of your monthly income to this expense item.

In addition, should no unforeseen financial contingencies arise during the month, you will have the satisfaction of recognizing your prudence and can increase the amount saved in the emergency fund, which over time could cover 6 to 12 months of essential expenses. You may find it useful for dealing with unexpected medical expenses, urgent repairs to your home or vehicle, or even to cover expenses when you find yourself in periods without a steady income, as may happen during a job loss or job transition.

It is strongly recommended that you keep your emergency fund intact and not use it for investments or other budget expenses. This fund should always be readily accessible in case of unforeseen situations. Avoiding affecting it will preserve its main function as a financial protection, providing you with a safety net in case of sudden needs.

A crucial aspect to consider is that establishing an emergency fund is not a whim, but rather an essential part of responsible financial management. Allocating an amount or a percentage of your income to deal with unforeseen expenses can give you considerable peace of mind, as you know you can cope with financial challenges when they arise. In addition, this approach teaches you to manage your money wisely in the long run, avoiding impulsive decisions or debt solutions that could jeopardize your financial stability.

It is important to note that the amount you allocate to this fund can vary greatly depending on your current financial situation. For example, if you have just started working or are on a limited income, you may not be able to immediately reserve 5 percent of your monthly income for this fund. In this case, you can start with a more modest percentage and gradually increase it as your income grows or your expenses decrease. The goal is to create a sustainable balance between creating the emergency fund and your other financial priorities.

## Tackle debt wisely

In recent years, the challenge of economic debt has become increasingly pressing, especially involving the young working population. Many young people are faced with a growing financial dilemma, pushed to the edge of a financial cliff by the constant increase in inspected expenses and unforeseen financial needs. This situation has prompted renewed attention to the dynamics of debt and the importance of dealing with it wisely.

Several interconnected factors combine to create an environment conducive to debt accumulation. Prominent among them are job insecurity, low wages and rising taxation. This explosive mix is further fueled by ever-increasing fixed expenses, which put a strain on anyone's budget, especially young people with limited financial resources. The influence of social media in setting living standards and personal image has added an additional layer of complexity to the financial management of young people.

The desire to conform to an idealized lifestyle, often conveyed through images of fashionable clothes, luxurious residences, and happy relationships, exerts a social pressure that is viable only through the acquisition of goods and services that are often beyond financial possibilities. This leads young people to consider recourse to debt as a pursued path to happiness.

At a time when the concept of ownership is giving way to a model of 'renting life', where everything from cars to household appliances is bought on instalments or leased, we are faced with compelling financial choices even at a young age.

Payments deferred over time may seem like an easy way to purchase goods or services that one cannot immediately afford. However, it is important to be aware of the potential risks these payments can entail. First, deferred payments are often associated with higher interest rates than payments made in one lump sum. This means that more money is spent in the long run to purchase the same good or service. Second, deferred payments can be difficult to manage if you are on a tight budget. If you are unable to make the monthly payments, you may risk incurring interest on late payments or being unable to take advantage of the good or service you purchased.

Third, deferred payments can lead to over-indebtedness. If you defer too many purchases, you can end up with a high level of debt, which can have a negative impact on your financial situation.

Here are some examples of how deferred payments can lead to financial problems in the future:

- Buying a new car with a high-interest loan. In the long run, you will spend much more on the car than you would pay for it with cash.

- Take a holiday trip with an instalment loan. If you lose your job or some other unforeseen event occurs, you may find yourself struggling to pay your pre-loan instalments.

- Making online purchases with a credit card in instalments. If you are unable to make your monthly payments, you may risk incurring interest charges or being unable to take advantage of the goods or services you have purchased.

To avoid future financial problems, it is important to carefully assess the risks associated with deferred payments before making a purchase. You should estimate your monthly costs and make sure you are able to make payments without eating into your budget and read the terms and conditions of the financing agreement carefully before signing it.

You should also compare the different types of financing available to find the one that best suits your needs.

If you are already in debt, it is critically important to get involved in reducing your economic debt as this helps to ensure greater financial stability and a more solid future. Reducing debt has a few direct benefits for your financial situation. First, it frees you from monthly financial burdens, allowing you to allocate more resources to your basic needs, savings and investments. In addition, reduced debt means less interest to pay in the long run, allowing you to save considerably on the total amount you would have to repay.

This savings power translates into greater financial flexibility, as you will have more resources available to meet unexpected expenses or to invest in future opportunities. Moreover, debt reduction improves your financial reliability, increasing your ability to access new loans or financing at more favorable rates. This becomes critically important both during emergency situations and for the realization of long-term financial goals, such as buying a home or financing your children's education.

Ultimately, engaging in economic debt reduction is a crucial step in creating a sound financial foundation, reducing financial stress, and ensuring greater freedom and opportunity in future financial choices.

The first step in the debt-reduction journey is to become aware of your debt situation. Make a list of all the debts you have, including the balance and interest rate for each. This will help you understand the extent of your debt and establish a plan of action.

The next step is to analyze your budget determine the monthly amount you will allocate to debt repayment. Once you have a clear view of your finances, set a reasonable goal for debt repayment.

One very effective approach is what is called the "Avalanche Effect." This is a debt repayment method that focuses on settling smaller debts before tackling larger ones. Basically, you start by directing additional payments toward the smallest debt while making minimum payments on the other debts. Once the smaller debt has been paid off, you use the amount previously allocated to that debt to ab- beat the next smaller debt and so on. This process creates a "snowball effect," in which the number of payments toward the debt gradually increases as the smaller debts are eliminated, accelerating the overall repayment process. This method aims not only to reduce debts faster, but also to create a sense of achievement and motivation along the way.

Maintain discipline and consistency in following your debt payment plan. Avoid accumulating more debt and try to cut non-essential expenses to free up more money for debt payment. If you feel overwhelmed, do not hesitate to seek help. Talk to a financial counsellor or debt expert to get advice and support in managing your financial situation. Remember: dealing with debt takes time and commitment. Do not look for quick or easy solutions, because they could lead to an even more difficult situation. Be patient and consistent in your approach to debt payment.

Finally, be kind to yourself. Debt may seem like a burden but remember that you are more than a sum of money. Focus on the progress you make in reducing debt and celebrate every step forward you take. Dealing with financial debt may seem difficult, but with careful planning, discipline and support, you can free yourself from debt and create a stronger financial foundation for your future. However, the choice to take on debt should not be demonized. When supported by proper financial education, debt can be used strategically to generate income when deployed wisely and well planned. This approach involves the use of external financing to take advantage of opportunities that might lead to gains greater than the cost of the debt itself.

An example of this is starting a new business venture. Borrowing money to start a business can allow investment in resources, equipment, and personnel, which in turn can generate profits. Instead of having to wait to put aside all the necessary capital, borrowing allows the business to start up more quickly and take advantage of market opportunities.

Another example is the acquisition of real estate for investment purposes. Borrowing money to buy a property to rent can generate passive income streams through monthly rents. If the income generated from rent exceeds the cost of debt and other as-associated expenses, a positive return on investment can be achieved.

In addition, debt can be used to finance training and personal development, which in turn can increase career opportunities and future income potential. However, it is critical to emphasize that using debt to generate income requires careful planning and realistic assessment of opportunities.

It is important to accurately calculate the cost of debt, consider potential risks and returns, and have a solid plan for repayment. Once again, we have evidence that financial education plays a foundational role in enabling people to make informed and responsible decisions about their finances.

## Avoid impulsive spending

In recent decades, the advent of technology and media has profoundly transformed our society and the way we shop. Today, more than ever before, we are constantly bombarded with public-target ads, special offers and promotions that seek to capture our attention and push us to purchase.

The Internet and social media have revolutionized the way we interact with brands and products. Online platform-forms offer a seamless shopping experience, allowing us to explore a wide range of products and services with just a few clicks. In addition, the pre-presence of algorithms that analyze our browsing interests and com-portions personalize the acquisition experience, presenting us with products that might be of greater interest.

This level of personalization increases the re-risk of impulse purchases, as we are exposed to content that reflects our individual preferences.

In addition, the availability of digital payment methods and quick delivery services has made purchases immediate and convenient. The aspect of instantaneousness has helped fuel the impulse to buy without thinking long about the financial consequences. Consumer culture has been amplified by the ease with which we can satisfy our material desires. The abundance of information online can also be deceptive. Positive reviews and rave testimonials can lead people to believe that a product is indispensable to their lives, even though it may not actually be.

However, it is worth pausing and pondering: how many of these enticing purchases are truly essential to our lives? What might seem like a worthwhile bargain at first may turn out to be a long-term cost to our financial stability. This phenomenon is known as compulsive shopping, a behavior that often affects young people in their 20s and 30s, just entering economic independence. That's why it is important to delve into this topic and find strategies to avoid falling into the trap of impulsive spending.

Imagine walking through the brightly lit aisles of a shopping center, surrounded by eye-catching promotions and objects that seem to beckon you. The excitement of a new purchase may trigger a momentary feeling of happiness, but soon the euphoria fades.

The true cost of impulsive buying is felt when moments of fleeting pleasure translate into an accumulated debt load that burdens our financial situation. It is therefore critical to learn to recognize the warning signs and develop strategies to avoid this vicious cycle.

Compulsive shopping is often associated with emotional impulses and anxieties. Especially young people, with their new economic independence but limited financial experience, may be particularly vulnerable to these reactions. The moment of happiness resulting from a purchase can easily turn into a silent addiction, masking any deeper discomforts.

A crucial approach to dealing with impulse spending is to adopt conscious and purposeful financial planning. This is not limited to creating a budget but requires critical analysis of short- and long-term financial goals. It is important to ask ourselves: what are the priorities? What do we really want to achieve from our financial independence? A well-structured plan helps us turn away from impulsive purchases and focus on what really matters to our financial well-being.

An effective approach to avoid impulsive spending is to ab-brace the 'rule of waiting'. When we feel the urge to make an impulsive purchase, it is helpful to stop. Let's give ourselves time to reflect and consider whether the purchase is necessary. Let's assign ourselves a waiting period of at least 24 hours, during which we can evaluate whether the purchase will maintain its appeal. Often, this pause helps us to see the object in question for what it is: a momentary temptation.

Changing the perspective, from immediate satisfaction to long-term benefits, is another powerful strategy for avoiding impulse spending. Imagine the satisfaction and pride that will come from having achieved our financial goals. A peaceful retirement, the realization of a dream home or a memorable travel experience will be far more valuable than any impulsive purchase.

## Look for bargains and discounts

If there is one golden rule in personal finance that young people under 40 should learn, it is to master the art of shopping wisely. In a world studded with irresistible offers and seemingly tempting discounts, it is crucial to develop the ability to discern between the real deal and the mere illusion of savings. When it comes to shopping, the key word is "research."

Having the patience to research, compare and evaluate diver-se options can make the difference between a well-considered shopping spree and an impulsive purchase. Use online resources, compare prices, read reviews, and seek advice from those with experience. Learning how to navigate deals and make the most of your money is a skill that will pay off over time.

Discounts and promotions are a common marketing strategy, but not all of them are truly beneficial. It is critical to develop a critical eye for evaluating the difference between a real discount and an illusion of savings. Always consider the original price of the product, read carefully the terms of the offer and consider whether the purchase is necessary. Sometimes, buying a product at a discount may still be more expensive than making a more considered choice.

Learning to evaluate the timing of purchases is another valuable skill. Not all periods are equal in terms of offers and discounts. Periods such as seasonal sales, Black Friday or Cyber Monday can offer unique opportunities to get quality products at bargain prices. However, remember that real savings are found in buying something you really need at a reduced price, not in accumulating useless items just because they are on sale.

While looking for bargains and discounts, it is essential to stick to your budget. It's easy to get caught up in the joy of discounts and end up spending more than you had budgeted. Before giving in to temptation, take a moment to consider whether the purchase is in line with your short- and long-term financial goals. A real bargain should not jeopardize your financial stability.

The difference between wise shopping and impulsive buying lies in the balance between desire and need. Ask yourself whether what you are considering buying will add value to your life. Satisfying a momentary desire may bring temporary gratification, but investing in something that improves the quality of your life in the long term is a wiser course of action.

# Chapter 4

# How to save money

Since ancient times, the accumulation of resources has been considered an act of wisdom. Ancient civilizations such as the Egyptians, Romans, and Greeks practiced rudimentary forms of saving by hoarding gold, silver, and other valuable resources. These assets represented a form of financial security and a way to cope with times of crisis or upheaval. The approach was often based on prudence and preparation for the future.

With the advent of the Industrial Revolution, the con-concept of saving underwent a significant transformation. Capital accumulation became crucial to finance rapidly expanding enterprises and support techno-technological innovation. The concept of investment became closely intertwined with savings, opening new opportunities for economic growth. Modern financial institutions, such as banks and stock exchanges, took shape, offering people new means to accumulate resources and participate in economic developments.

Major economic crises, such as the Great Depression of 1929, reinforced the perception of saving as a means of livelihood. Households that had saved money or accumulated resources during periods of prosperity had a safety net during financial storms. These events underscored the need for prudent financial management and the building of emergency reserves.

In the modern era, globalization has made the financial world more interconnected than ever before. Opportunities for savings and investment have multiplied, but this has also introduced new challenges. Financial education has become crucial for making informed decisions and avoiding excessive risk. In this context, saving has been recognized as the foundation on which to build a sound financial base before taking riskier actions, such as investing in volatile markets. It is intriguing to observe how economic theories have influenced our view of savings and how we can concretize these ideas in our everyday lives.

As an example, Rational Consumer Theory tells us that consumers make rational decisions by trying to maximize their subjective utility. This concept has led to an increased focus on saving as a means of achieving greater future utility. For example, an individual might forego impulsive spending to purchase a durable good that brings more long-term value.

The income effect theory suggests that an increase in income leads to an increase in consumption, but not in pro-portion. This concept has led many people to re-spend some of the increased income instead of spending all of it immediately. For example, if a per-person receives a salary increase, he or she might decide to allocate a percentage of that increase to saving an- rather than spending it all.

The life-cycle perspective proposes that per-sons plan their consumption and savings over their lifetime, considering changes in income at different ages. This can influence financial decisions such as retirement planning and saving for future events. For example, an individual might decide to save more when he or she is young to ensure a comfortable retirement in old age.

And again, the diminishing marginal utility model suggests that each additional unit of a good offers less utility than previous units. This can influence consumption and savings choices, prompting people to carefully evaluate the balance between immediate satisfaction and saving for the future.

Economic theories offer a more appropriate understanding of saving and its implications. By taking these perspectives into account in our financial decisions, we can make more in-formed financial decisions that will help us achieve our goals.

Saving is not just putting money aside. It is a mindset that pushes you to be more mindful of your spending, to look for ways to save, and to make informed financial decisions. This practice is critical for realizing aspirations, dealing with unexpected situations, and co-building a financial safety net. Consider saving as an investment in yourself, rather than as a restriction, a means that offers you the financial freedom to face the future with confidence and to shape the life you want

We have already seen how easy it is nowadays to fall into the traps of impulsive consumerism, letting expenses pile up without careful thought. But take a moment to imagine how you might turn your financial approach on its head.

You might ask yourself, "Why should I care? Can't I just enjoy my earnings now?" No doubt, enjoying life and indulging in small joys is wonderful, but saving offers benefits that span the long term. In practical terms, this involves allocating a portion of your income to reserve instead of spending it entirely.

Saving can be difficult at first, but the benefits that come with it are many. One of the most important is financial security. Setting aside some of your income provides you with a financial lifesaver that helps you meet un-anticipated expenses such as car repairs or medical bills, without having to resort to borrowing. And when these situations arise, as they inevitably will, the feeling of security and tranquility you will experience will be priceless.

But saving is not just a matter of readiness for emergencies. It also allows you to build capital that brings you closer to your dreams and ambitions. Whether you decide to travel, buy a house or start your own business, constant saving will help you accumulate the de-money needed to achieve these goals.

Another benefit of saving is its ability to develop financial discipline. This practice will teach you to manage money more effectively and make wiser financial decisions, reducing the risk of complicated situations related to debt and overspending.

In addition, saving grants you the freedom to make more informed financial decisions. When you have an emergency fund and are accumulating resources for your future goals, you have the luxury of taking the time to examine your options and make thoughtful decisions.

This protects you from the risk of hasty or impulsive choices that could have negative consequences for your financial well-being. Myths and mistaken beliefs often surround the concept of re-spending. Some associate it with deprivation, as if having to give up expensive dinners out or entertainment is a necessity. But it is not. Saving does not represent deprivation, but rather a choice that directs your energy toward what really matters.

Nor is it true that saving limits your social life and sources of entertainment. On the contrary, saving helps you distinguish between momentary desires and long-term needs, embrace delayed gratification, and gain a broader, more conscious perspective. It is a journey of self-knowledge that will lead you to a financial future in which your choices will be governed by awareness, not impulsivity.

## The savings mindset

When it comes to saving, it is critical to have the mental approach that will help you overcome challenges and maintain motivation in the long run. Cultivate positive thinking about saving. See it as an opportunity, a way to achieve your financial goals. Focus on what you are gaining through saving rather than what you are giving up.

A crucial point is to set clear financial goals; achieve them through saving. Knowing why you are saving and what outcome you want to achieve gives you concrete direction. This could be buying a house, a trip, or a solid retirement fund. These goals act as tangible motivators and help you stay focused.

Also, embrace a long-term perspective. This involves shifting the focus from immediate gratifications to those that develop over time. Instead of seeking satisfaction through impulsive purchases, focus your attention on the positive effects saving will have on your financial security and ability to fulfil your desires. While the world pushes for instant gratification, long-term thinking pushes us to consider financial consequences over time. This involves avoiding unnecessary spending and focusing on goals we consider priority, such as owning a home, investing in education or co-building a secure retirement.

In addition to looking far ahead, the savings mindset requires the ability to make informed choices. It means understanding that every expenditure is a choice that impacts our overall financial situation. This prompts us to carefully assess priorities and focus on the things that really matter.

We learn to say "no" to expenses that do not add value to our lives and to say "yes" to opportunities that bring us closer to our goals.

Automate saving to make it a habit. Set up an automatic transfer of your income into a savings account. This allows you to set aside money before you face expenses, making saving a priority.

Another crucial aspect is an appreciation for gradual progress. Too often we focus on the big steps forward, neglecting the small progress that brings us closer to our goals. The savings mentality teaches us to recognize and celebrate every step forward, no matter how seemingly modest. This strengthens our resolve and helps us stay focused on our goal without letting ourselves become discouraged.

Try to embrace frugality. It means finding smart ways to save money without sacrifice. It might mean cooking at home instead of eating out, looking for deals and discounts, or reducing waste.

Financial agility is another central aspect of the savings mindset. Because life is full of unforeseen events and financial challenges can arise at any time, adopting a flexible approach allows us to deal with situations more efficiently, without having to resort to debt. We learn to manage expenses intelligently, making regular adjustments when necessary.

Finally, harness your thirst for financial knowledge and awareness. Being educated about financial dynamics allows us to make more informed decisions. This makes you an active player in managing your finances, rather than a passive spectator. Being aware of the options available to you allows you to develop more effective re-spending strategies that can adapt to changing market conditions and your changing needs

Developing this right mental approach to saving takes time and practice to develop, but once you have internalized it, it can guide you toward greater financial stability and a more secure future.

## Cut unnecessary spending

On the path to savings, it is crucial to examine unnecessary expenses that can silently erode your financial resources. Identifying these areas of waste is the first step in adopting a financially sustainable lifestyle.

Undoubtedly, entertainment, meals out, subscriptions, and impulse purchases add a touch of pleasure to life. However, it is important to consider how these expenses can affect our ability to save. When we regularly indulge in expensive entertainments or give in to the lure of meals out, we gradually subtract resources from our budget, leaving little or no money available for savings.

Subscription services, which offer unlimited access to content, products or services for a fixed price, are increasingly popular. The desire for novelty and special offers drives many people to take out subscriptions, without considering that they may not use them regularly, thus accumulating costs that could instead be destined for savings.

This is also true of most impulse purchases: although they may provide momentary satisfaction, they can have a major impact on our finances in the long run.

All this is not to say that we should eliminate these pleasurable aspects from our lives, but rather find a balance between them and more demanding activities. With greater awareness of our spending and judicious planning, we can still enjoy these experiences without compromising our ability to save. The key is to find a balance between spending for immediate pleasure and saving for the future.

There are numerous tactics you can adopt to re-spend money and move forward toward your financial goals:

- Thoughtful choices: Evaluate your spending considering your values and financial goals. Focus on what truly enriches your life and consider phasing out expenses that do not add value.

- Plan Purchases: Avoid impulse purchases. Before making a purchase, give yourself time to think about whether it is necessary and whether It will contribute to your long-term well-being.

- Creative Alternatives: Explore alternatives for entertainment and food, such as home evenings with friends or cooking delicious meals at home.

- Review Subscriptions: Review the monthly subscriptions you have. You may find that some of them are no longer needed or that there are cheaper options.

- Energy Awareness: Reduce energy waste, not only for the environmental benefit, but also to save on your utility bill.

- Beware of Minimal Expenses: Small, trivial expenses can pile up. Watch your daily outgoings carefully and think about where you can apply changes.

- Research and Compare: Before making major purchases, compare prices and look for advantageous deals. Even a little research can lead to significant savings.

- Choose Value: Change your perspective on purchases. Look for experiences and items that bring real value to your life instead of accumulating superficial goods.

- Gradual Progress: Reducing superfluous expenses does not require drastic change. Focus on your financial goals and take small but steady steps toward a more sustainable lifestyle.

Cutting unnecessary expenses is not about sacrificing pleasure or experiences. Rather, it is about adjusting your spending habits to align with your financial priorities. Through wise decisions and well-defined strategies, you can create a balance between enjoying the present and building a solid financial future.

## Automatic savings strategies

Automatic savings strategies allow you to stabilize a routine in which a percentage of your income is automatically set aside. It's like building a castle brick by brick, without having to deal with the burden of doing it all at once.

But there's more: these strategies are flexible. You can choose to dedicate a small percentage or a fixed amount each month. This gives you control over how much you are saving, tailoring it to your needs and goals.

In addition, you can gradually increase the percentage as your financial situation improves, without feeling the burden.

In addition, automatic saving is a silent ally against temptation. When money is auto saved into a separate account, it becomes more difficult to spend it impulsively. This helps you maintain discipline and avoid unnecessary waste. In addition, you could focus on living in the present, knowing that your financial future is already preserved.

Here are some possible strategies for automatized savings:

- Automatic withdrawal: Set up a regular withdrawal from your checking account to your savings account.

- Transaction rounding: Round each transaction to the next dollar and set the difference aside.

- Deduction from salary: Ask your employer to deduct a portion of your salary and deposit it directly into a savings account.

- Automatic investments: Set up recurring investment plans to buy stocks, funds or other financial instruments.

All these strategies can be traced back to the particularly effective concept of "pay yourself first" first expressed by George S. Clason in his book entitled "The Richest Man in Babylon." This technique challenges the traditional order of things. Instead of waiting for all your expenses to be met and then saving what is left over, you commit yourself to setting aside a percentage of your income at the as a tribute to your future prosperity. It is like paying tribute to yourself and your financial goals before everything else.

But why should you do this? Because "paying yourself first" changes your approach to spending. When you pay yourself first, you set a clear limit to your spending, forcing you to live within your means. This challenges you to be creative with your budget and look for ways to maximize the value of your spending. It is an opportunity to discover how to live well on less, freeing you from the illusion that more spending means more satisfaction.

## Dream, save, achieve

I bet you have dreams and goals in your life, right? And you know what? Saving is a powerful ally that will help you realize those dreams and ensure your long-term economic security. It may not sound as exciting as spending money on fun things but let me tell you why saving is so important.

When you save with a specific goal in mind, you transcend mere money conservation. Emergencies, inevitable in life, become less frightening when you have a financial safety net to draw on. Investments stop being abstract and become tools that can bring projects and dreams to life. Your personal aspirations, which might seem unattainable, become more tangible when you assemble resources to achieve them.

But there's more: saving for specific goals teaches you the power of focus. When you have a clear goal in mind, you become more careful about your spending and the opportunities that can bring you closer to the finish line. This challenges you to be selective with your choices and to concentrate on the priorities that really matter to you.

Moreover, this approach embodies a fundamental principle: money is a means to your ends, not an end. Saving for specific goals pushes you to think about what you really want and how you can create value in your life. It is a way to bring your dreams to life in a purposeful way, without falling into the trap of impulsive spending or a financial routine empty of meaning-to.

Imagine you have a gym membership. If you don't work out regularly, the result will be less noticeable and you won't reach your fitness goals, right? Well, saving works much the same way. Setting aside a portion of your income each month is like training-your money to achieve important financial goals.

Setting savings goals is an important step in managing your personal finances.

The first step is to think about what you really want in your life. You may want to travel to faraway places, buy your first car, or start your own business. Perhaps you have a long-term dream, such as buying a house or saving to pay for your studies at a prestigious university. Whether big or small, your goals are an important guide for your savings strategy.

Once you're clear on what you want to achieve, it's time to get specific. Vague goals like "save money" do not work well. You need to be detailed in de-defining your goals. For example, instead of saying "save-re for a vacation," you can specify "save 1,000 dollars for a vacation to Europe by the end of the year." That makes your goal more concrete and measurable.

Another important aspect is to set a time frame for achieving your goals. You may want to save up for a birthday gift or a trip within a month. Other goals may take longer, such as saving for college, which could take years. Setting a deadline will help you maintain focus and measure your progress.

Let's start with your short-term goals. These are goals you want to achieve within a few months or within a year. They could be things like saving for a small vacation, buying a special gift for someone, or buying an item you have wanted for a long time. Short-term goals are achievable in a relatively short period and will give you great satisfaction when you achieve them.

Now let's move on to medium-term goals. These are goals that you would like to accomplish within one or two years. It could be saving for a bigger trip, changing your smartphone, or enrolling in a course or training that interests you. Medium-term goals require a little more time and planning, but they are co-maybe quite accessible in the short term.

Finally, we have the long-term goals. These are your biggest dreams, which you wish to achieve over the course of several years or ad- even a lifetime. It could be-buy a house, start your own business, or save-re for college or your retirement. Long-term goals require more in-depth planning and constant commitment, but they are the ones that will give you the greatest rewards.

Whenever you set a goal, ask yourself which of the three categories it falls into. This will help you set clear milestones and plan the steps needed to achieve it. You might want to save 100 dollars a month for the short-term trip, 200 dollars a month for the medium-term course, and 500 dollars a month for the long-term project. Breaking down your goals into these categories will give you a clearer picture of your finances and help you prioritize. You may want to focus first on short-term goals, because they give you immediate gratification, and then move on to medium- and long-term goals, because they re-require longer planning.

Remember that goals should be realistic and achievable. You cannot save thousands in a set-week, so be honest with yourself about the time and resources you have available. Break your goals down into small steps and celebrate each milestone along the way.

The next step is to figure out how much you will need to save each month to reach your goals. If your goal is to save 1,000 dollars within 10 months, you will need to set aside 100 dollars each month. This planning will help you understand if your goal is realistic and give you a concrete plan to follow.

When you set savings goals, it is also important to monitor your progress. This will help you stay motivated and keep your focus on your financial goals. But how can you keep track of your progression?

One of the most effective strategies is to keep a log or diary of your finances. You can use a notebook or app to record all your income and expenses. Record each transaction and add a brief note about the o-goal with which it is associated. In this way, you will have a complete panoramic of your financial situation and be able to monitor your progress toward your savings goals.

Another useful strategy is to create a visual chart or graph. You can draw it by hand or use online tools to create a chart of your finances. For example, you can track the growth of your emergency fund over the months or see how your savings are growing toward a specific goal. A graph will give you a clear visual representation of your progress and give you greater motivation to continue.

If you prefer a more technological approach, there are numerous apps available to manage your finances and track your savings. These apps allow you to link your bank accounts, categorize your expenses, and track your budget. Many of them also offer goal-tracking features, so you can see how close you are to your financial dreams.

Another idea is to involve a friend or family member in your savings journey. Talk to someone you trust about your financial goals and ask them to be your "savings buddy." You could compare your progress and support each other when you feel a little demotivated.

Finally, keep in mind that it is normal to have ups and downs in your savings journey. There will be times when you find it difficult to save and others when you will reach important milestones. Don't get discouraged if you don't reach your goals right away. What matters is maintaining discipline and continuing to take small steps toward your financial dreams.

Keeping track of progress toward achieving your savings goals will help you stay focused and motivated in your financial journey. Choose the strategy that me- best fits your needs and make it part of your financial routine. With perseverance and commitment, you'll see results and realize your dreams in no time.

A strong driver to activate whenever your determination to save begins to wane is to visualize the long-term value of the money you save. Imagine a scenario in which you save 100 dollars a month for 5 years. This commitment results in 6,000 dollars after 10 years and 14,000 dollars after 20 years, thanks to the effect of compound interest.

Now, think about increasing your savings to 200 dollars per month for 30 years. This constant effort would lead to a remarkable result: more than 100,000 dollars. This important amount provides you with tangible evidence that patience and perseverance in saving can lead to truly significant financial results. Adopting a time perspective can factually inspire more forward-looking financial actions and transform the idea of saving from a semi-simple act of giving up to an investment in yourself and your financial future.

## Smart savings: from small to large expenses

Every day we face a variety of expenses: from coffee at the bar to shopping for lunch out, and it all seems so irresistible. But you know what? There are smart ways to reduce your daily expenses and save that money for more important things.

First, take a moment to think about what your most frequent daily expenses are. They might be meals out, impulse purchases or subscriptions you never use. Identifying these expenses will help you figure out where you can start saving money.

A simple but effective strategy is to carry a reusable water bottle with you. Buying water every day may seem small, but at the end of the month it can add up to a significant amount. Reducing these small expenses will save you money and will also help re-reduce plastic pollution.

Another way to reduce daily expenses is to plan meals at home and cook. Eating out can be expensive, especially if you do it often. Preparing meals at home will save you money and give you the opportunity to choose healthier and tastier ingredients. In addition to cooking, you can also take your lunch to work or school instead of buying it. Packing a packed lunch will save you a lot of money in the long run and allow you to better control what you eat.

Turn off lights when you are not using them and unplug electrical appliances from the outlet when you are not using them. The standby current of many household appliances can accumulate and account for a significant part of the bill. Use energy-saving led bulbs and try to wash clothes with cold water if possible. Also, consider in-stalling a programmable thermostat to regulate the temperature in your home and save on heating and cooling energy.

Another way to save money is to reduce hot water use. Prefer showers to baths and consider installing water-saving devices, such as low-flow faucets. You can also harvest rainwater to water plants, thus reducing your use of potable water and its impact on the environment.

Regarding utility bills, an important strategy is to compare rates and services for utility bills co-meaning insurance, electricity, or internet. You can utilize websites or apps that compare prices to find the best deals on the market.

Buy in bulk when there are deals and use coupons or loyalty cards to get discounts on the pro-ducts you buy regularly.

When you want to shop online, leave your order in the shopping cart for a few days before finalizing your purchase. you may find that your urge to buy that product will be gone and you will save money. Also, search the web for discount codes and promotions before making payment.

Occasionally, give yourself a "no-spend day." Impost one day a week or month where you commit to spending nothing. You will find that you can survive without those impulse purchases and that savings are possible.

Every little saving action count, and over time, your efforts will be rewarded. You may have heard of the cumulative effect. It may sound like a complicated term, but it is actually a very simple and potent concept. The cumulative effect refers to the idea that small actions or changes you make daily can have a significant impact in the long run.

Every time you avoid buying a bottle of ac- water at the bar, pack your lunch at home instead of buying it, or find an offer on a product you want, you are setting aside a small amount of money that adds up and grows over time. The key to making the most of the cumulative effect is consistency and perseverance. Small daily re-saving actions may seem insignificant on their own, but when you repeat them and make them into habits, they will have a huge impact in the long run.

In order to deal effectively with the financial challenges associated with significant expenses, such as buying a car or a house, it is imperative to put an emphasis on saving and the ability to distinguish between wants and real needs.

Buying a shiny car or realizing the dream of owning a cozy home can generate a kind of euphoria. But resisting the initial excitement and looking at financial matters rationally and thoughtfully is a key step towards achieving one's financial goals.

Especially when it comes to relevant investments, careful research forms the basis. Take the time to explore the various options available to you, carefully evaluating the details of each. This patient investigation will not only help you make more in-formed decisions but will guard you against hasty choices that you may later regret.

When it comes to automobiles, the decision between a new and a used model requires a few evaluations to be made. While a new car might appeal to you because of its freshness, it is crucial to reflect on the fact that new cars experience significant depreciation in the first few years. A smart alternative might be a used car in excellent condition, which offers an attractive compromise between quality and cost.

About the purchase of a property, it must be borne in mind that the decision goes beyond mere convenience.

In addition to your current needs, consider the future growth of your family, potential changes in your career, and your financial goals. Also, consider buying in up-and-coming neighborhoods, which could offer a long-term investment through rising property values.

But the analysis should not be limited to the purchase price. Deal honestly with short- and long-term costs. For a car, consider the cost of maintenance, insurance, and fuel. For a house, consider taxes, ma-maintenance expenses, and utilities. These elements, often overlooked, can greatly affect your monthly budget and should be included in your overall assessment.

If you have the option, consider a more substantial initial payment. This will not only reduce your debt, but also the amount of interest in the long run. The result will be significant savings over the years and greater financial peace of mind.

Negotiation also takes on an important role. Do not be afraid to look for a better price, whether you are negotiating with a car dealer or a real estate seller. Learning the art of negotiation will not only save you money, but will give you a sense of control over your financial situation. However, the heart of this strategy is financial planning. Start by setting clear and reason-able goals. Determine the total costs of the purchase, including initial and recurring costs, and once you have this in-formation, create a structured savings plan.

In some cases, it may come in handy to open an account dedicated to your goal. Keeping your savings separate will help you avoid temptation and allow you to monitor progress in a more tangible way. Also consider using term accounts, which prevent you from touching your savings until the maturity date.

## The jar method

There are several techniques that can be adopted to save money. One of the most effective draws on folk wisdom.

Our grandmothers often used a simple but effective method to manage their finances: the "jar" system. This technique consisted of dividing the money into several jars, each labelled with a specific expenditure item. Each time they received an income, they would assign a specific amount of money to each jar according to their financial priorities.

For example, they could have one jar for food expenses, one for bills, one for transportation, one for entertainment, and so on. This system helped people keep track of their spending, prevent overuse of funds, and ensure that each expense item had its portion of the budget.

This practice had several advantages. First, it ensured that fixed expenses, such as rent or utility bills, were-always covered, preventing financial problems. In addition, it co-stressed people to plan carefully for discretionary expenses, such as entertainment or shopping, since the money available in that jar had to last until the next budget period.

This method of money management promoted greater awareness of spending, helping to avoid waste and save for future needs. Although it may seem like a traditional approach, many of the lessons applied from this practice can still be applied today for responsible financial management.

Whenever you receive income, consider splitting funds into dedicated "containers," an idea that can be easily accomplished today through digital solutions as well. Many banks, in fact, provide the functionality to subdivide your checking account into sub-accounts, allowing you to assign specific funds to different spending categories. This practice allows you to manage your pay checks digitally, offering the same convenience as traditional "barter."

You might choose to put a fixed percentage of your income into each pay check or establish specific amounts for each category. This strategy requires a good deal of discipline and awareness of your spending. You must stick to your savings plan and set aside money for each category. But with a little effort, you will see results over time.

Remember that there is no one-size-fits-all strategy. You can adapt this technique according to your personal needs and preference. The important thing is to understand what your financial goals are and choose the savings strategy that best fits your needs.

Saving is an important skill to build a solid foundation for your financial future. With patience and consistency, this savings strategy will help you develop healthier financial habits and achieve your goals.

## Meeting the challenges of saving

Maintaining motivation to save can be a challenge, especially when facing financial difficulties. But don't worry, because with determination and commitment you can overcome these challenges and continue to pursue your financial goals.

One of the keys to maintaining motivation is to always keep in mind why you are saving. Ask yourself: what are your financial goals? What do you want to achieve with your savings? It may be buying a house, traveling, creating an emergency fund, or preparing for retirement. Keeping your goals in mind will help you stay focused and overcome temptations to spend impulsively.

Also, remember that saving does not have to be a total sacrifice. You can give yourself small rewards from time to time to keep your motivation high. For example, after you reach an important savings goal, you can afford an outing with friends or a re-gal that you have been longing for. These rewards will encourage you to continue the savings path.

Another strategy for maintaining motivation is to try to make saving fun and engaging. Involve friends or family members in your savings goal and organize challenges or games to see who can save the most. You could also keep a journal of your progress and write down your successes and goals achieved. This will help you see how much you have already accomplished and encourage you to continue.

Finally, don't be afraid to ask for help. If you find yourself in a difficult financial situation, talk to a trusted person, such as a friend, family member or financial advisor. Sharing your thoughts and concerns will help you develop new perspectives and find solutions to your problems.

When it comes to saving money, it is inevitable that along the way there will be unforeseen events and obstacles that undermine your financial efforts. However, it is important not to let this get you down. Try to approach financial problems with a positive and proactive mindset. Rather than seeing yourself as a victim of circumstances, take control of your financial situation and seek creative solutions to overcome difficulties. Facing these situations with a positive mindset and appropriate strategies will help you overcome them successfully and continue to pursue your savings goals.

Another important aspect is to be flexible with your savings plan. You may face unanticipated expenses that force you to deviate temporarily from your savings plans. Do not be discouraged by this; it is perfectly normal. The important thing is to get back on track as soon as the situation allows.

In addition, it is essential to regularly review one's budget and expenditure. Sometimes, there may be superfluous expenses that can be cut or reduced to free up more money for savings. Keep a close eye on your finances and try to do regular "check-ups" to make sure you are on track with your savings goals.

## Financial instruments

Talking about financial tools for savings is a crucial topic for anyone who wants to manage their finances wisely. There are several options that can help you grow your money over time and achieve your financial goals.

One of the first tools I recommend that you considerate is the savings account. This is a very simple but effective tool for keeping your savings safe and earning some interest. Many savings accounts offer competitive interest rates and allow you to accumulate your savings at any time.

If you are willing to invest your savings longer term, you may consider certificates of deposit (CDs) or government bonds. CDs are like savings accounts, but they require that your money remain deposited for a specific period of time. In return, you get a higher interest rate than in a traditional savings account. Government bonds, on the other hand, are low-risk investments issued by the government and offer stable returns.

Another financial instrument that can be useful for saving is the retirement savings plan (Pension Fund). This type of investment helps you prepare for the future by allowing you to accumulate money for pension with regular contributions.

When it comes to choosing financial instruments for savings, it is important to carefully assess one's needs, level of risk and financial goals. Before making any investment, take the time to inform yourself and fully understand the features and risks of each financial instrument.

# Chapter 5

# How to protect money

Our focus is often on accumulating money and growing it, but it is equally essential to comprehend how to protect it from the unforeseen pitfalls that life may hold. Imagine for a moment that you are a co-builder of sandcastles on the beach. You have invested time and effort in creating majestic structures, representative of your financial ambitions. However, just when your castle seems solid, an unexpected and threatening wave arrives. Without adequate protection, your work can be lost in an instant.

Saving and investing are certainly important, but what makes your financial strategy truly resilient is the ability to withstand unforeseen events, such as unexpected average expenses, job loss, or fluctuations in the financial markets. Protecting your money means being prepared to meet these challenges without jeopardizing your overall financial stability, and to do so, it is important to have a comprehensive view of the potential threats that could put it at risk.

Throughout this chapter, we will explore how to affront these financial pitfalls, discovering different protection options that fit your needs, but keep in mind that financial protection is not an occasional update, but a key part of your overall financial journey.

## The invisible enemy

In an environment of increasing digitization, cyber breaches are an increasingly significant risk. These incidents occur when hackers manage to infiltrate the systems of companies, financial institutions, or online organizations, stealing personal information such as email addresses, passwords, credit card details, and bank account numbers. Cybercriminals are making use of advanced hacking methodologies to infiltrate computer systems. Among these, the technique known as phishing is gaining ground. This is a type of in-form attack that involves sending fake messages or emails, ostensibly from authoritative sources, but aimed at obtaining personal or financial information.

Once in possession of your data, individuals with malicious intent can exploit your personal information to gain access to your financial accounts and conduct unauthorized transactions. These actions could include opening bank accounts, loan applications or purchases in your name, potentially resulting in damaging your credit reputation and causing significant financial losses. In some cases, they can go so far as to directly steal your money, literally making it disappear from your online checking account.

It is therefore critical to take security measures to protect our sensitive data, such as using complex passwords that are replaced regularly, and to avoid inferring personal information from unsecure websites.

In order to prevent online threats, it is also advisable to install and keep up-to-date good antivirus software on the devices used for financial transactions. This will protect against malware and other threats.

In addition, when conducting financial transactions online, it is critical to use safe and secure Internet connections and avoid conducting financial transactions over public or unsecured Wi-Fi networks.

Another common situation is scam e-mails. To avoid them, it is important to be vigilant and always verify the authenticity of the sender, especially if they come from well-known financial institutions or companies. In general, it is best to avoid clicking on suspicious links or entering personal information in response to suspicious e-mails.

By following these tips, you can reduce the risk of falling victim to financial fraud and protect personal and financial in-formation more effectively.

## Insurance for everyday life

While cyber threats often occupy the titles of the headlines, there are also real-world threats that can significantly compromise your financial stability. These threats range from medical emergencies to automobile accidents, from job loss to liability situations.

A young person like you, committed to building assets, may suddenly find himself or herself grappling with unexpected expenses that put a strain on accumulated financial resources. A traffic accident can cause considerable property damage and generate claims for compensation. In addition, job loss, especially in times of economic instability, can lead to a drop in income and influence the ability to save and invest.

Another aspect that is often overlooked is liability, which can result from accidents or unintentional injury to third parties. This threat could result in legal costs and financial compensation that can erode assets accumulated over time. It is therefore vital to have adequate insurance coverage to protect against such situations.

In Chapter Three, we previously examined how the presence of a robust and easily accessible emergency fund acts as an effective financial cushion. This fund provides adequate resources to deal with unexpected expenses, such as job loss or medical emergencies, without having to resort to borrowing or going into debt. Moreover, using the various insurance options available can be an important defense against this type of threat. Insurance such as health, life, and property insurance can offer crucial support in times of need, enabling you to deal with difficult situations without having to bear the entire financial burden alone.

## Protection from economic crises

Economic crises can have a significant impact on assets and personal finances. These periods of financial turbulence can cause a number of consequences that affect people's economic stability. Here are some ways in which economic crises can affect personal wealth and finances:

- Loss of income: During economic crises, many companies reduce their activities or close down completely, causing job and income losses. Unemployment the reduction of working hours can lead to a decrease in family income, making it difficult to meet daily expenses to maintaining one's standard of life.

- Debt and non-payment: With the loss of income, many people may find themselves unable to meet their debts and financial obligations. This can lead to late payments on loans, credit cards and bills, causing further financial problems and damage to creditworthiness.

- Decline in the value of investments: Economic crises often result in a decline in the value of investments, such as stocks, bonds, and mutual funds. This can have a negative impact on the net worth of people who depend on investments for their long-term financial growth.

- Decrease in property value: During crises, the real estate market can decline, leading to a reduction in property values. This can have a direct impact on the assets of people who own real estate or who are mortgage holders.

- Increased cost of borrowing: To cope with crises, banks and financial institutions may increase interest rates on loans, making access to credit more expensive. This can make it difficult to obtain financing for major purchases or investments.

- Reduced consumer confidence: Crises undermine consumer confidence. This can lead to reduced spending, whether on purchases of luxury goods or necessities. The diminution in consumer spending can in turn affect overall economic activity.

- Withdrawal from pensions: Some people may be forced to withdraw part of their pension or instalments in order to cope with financial difficulties due to an economic crisis. This could have a negative impact on long-term financial security.

Investment allocation and diversification are two key strategies for mitigating the impact of economic crises on wealth and personal finances. Both play a substantial role in balancing risk and potential growth in the investment portfolio.

More specifically, investment allocation refers to the division of the investment portfolio into different asset categories, such as stocks, bonds, real estate, and cash. This division is done according to the investor's financial objectives, acceptable risk level, and risk profile. During economic crises, some assets may be more affected than others. For example, stocks may experience sharp declines, while bonds may be less volatile. Proper investment allocation can help reduce the negative impact of a single declining asset class, as the performance of different categories offset each other

Diversification is a crucial part of investment allocation. It involves investing in a broad spectrum of assets within each asset class. For example, instead of investing in a single stock, one could invest in a portfolio of stocks from different companies and sectors. This reduces the risk associated with a single investment that could be negatively affected by specific corporate events. Diversification helps to balance portfolio risk, as the loss of a single system will have less impact on a fully diversified portfolio.

These strategies aim to minimize risk and increase the resilience of the portfolio to financial shocks: However, it is important to note c and no strategy can completely eliminate the risk of losses during crises. Therefore, it is advisable to seek the advice of financial experts and regularly review your portfolio to adapt it to changes in market and financial objectives.

Asset diversification

An individual's financial assets can be subdivided into different forms, each of which represents a specific component of his or her overall complex financial situation. These forms of assets include:

- Cash: This category includes cash, bank accounts, liquid savings, and other easily accessible assets that can be used for everyday expenses or emergencies.

- Investments: These are assets such as stocks, bonds, mutual funds, government bonds and other financial investments that can generate returns over time.

- Real estate: This type of business includes real estate such as houses, land, apartments, offices, or other properties that may have appreciable value over time.

- Entrepreneurial assets: Entrepreneurs may have financial assets related to their business activities, which may include assets, shareholdings or company shares.

- Personal Assets: This category includes valuables such as jewelry, artwork, vehicles, and other personal assets that may contribute to the overall wealth.

Financial assets held in the form of cash may be subject to various financial threats that compromise their security and value over time. One such threat is inflation, a phenomenon characterized by rising prices of goods and services. When inflation is high, the amount of goods that can be purchased with a given amount of money decreases over time.

Another threat involves low interest rates. When banks offer low yields on re-mortgage accounts or term deposits, the potential de-revenue from cash is limited. This can affect the growth of financial assets in the long run. Storing too much cash can also lead to a loss of real value. If cash is not invested or used, its value may decrease over time due to the absence of significant returns.

Moreover, holding large amounts of cash can entail security risks. Theft or loss of cash could result in large financial losses with no possibility of recovery.

Another important aspect is exposure to fi-scale evasion. In some cases, holding significant amounts of cash may raise suspicions of tax evasion by tax authorities, leading to possible investigation or penalties.

To counter these threats, it is essential to balance the amount of cash held with other forms of investment. Diversifying the portfolio, seeking investment opportunities that offer a balance between risk and return, and adopting prudent financial management can help protect financial assets over time.

Savings invested in financial instruments are exposed to several risks that can impair their value. One such threat is volatility in financial markets. Fluctuations in the prices of stocks, bonds, and other financial instruments can cause significant losses for investors, especially in times of economic turbulence.

Another threat is related to poor portfolio diversification. Concentrating investments in only one set-tore or asset class can increase the risk of loss if that sector experiences a downturn. Lack of diversification can result in high exposure to negative events that could affect the complex value of assets.

Choosing complex and poorly understood financial products is another threat. Investing in financial instruments that are too complex can lead to excessive risk and a lack of understanding of possible financial outcomes. This can lead to in-gent losses and a lack of control over one's assets.

Lack of flexibility in dealing with market developments can also be a potential threat to one's assets. Developments in financial markets can vary based on multiple factors, including economic, political, and social events. Investors should be prepared to review and adjust their investment strategies accordingly. Finally, ignoring the costs associated with investments can harm financial assets. High commissions, management fees, and other fees can erode overall returns over time.

To address these threats, a thoughtful and diversified investment strategy is essential. Research and understanding of financial instruments, regular monitoring of markets, and advice from financial professionals can help make informed decisions and protect financial assets from excessive risk.

Real estate is an important component of an individual's financial assets, but it is exposed to several financial dangers that require attention and precautions. One such threat is the depreciation of real estate values. Fluctuations in the real estate market can affect the value of a property over time, leading to a decrease in the value of the investment.

Another threat is related to maintenance and the expenses associated with the property. Lack of maintenance can lead to high costs for repairs and renovations, which can erode the value of the investment in the long run. Fixed expenses such as property taxes and condominium fees can affect the financial returns associated with the property.

The inability to find reliable tenants can rap-present another threat. If a property is not rented or if rents are not paid on a regular basis, the investor may suffer significant financial losses. In addition, changes in the rental market can affect the profitability of real estate investment.

Fluctuations in interest rates can affect the financing costs of the property. If interest rates rise, mortgage costs may increase, influencing the profitability of the investment. On the other hand, lower interest rates may encourage the purchase of property, but may carry risks related to future rate trends.

Finally, general economic conditions can affect the supply and demand for real estate. During periods of economic recession, demand for property may decrease, affecting the timing of sales and property prices.

To reduce the financial risks associated with real estate investment, it is important to carefully research the market and area in which you intend to invest, carefully evaluate the costs associated with purchasing, maintaining, and operating the property, insure against natural and maintenance risks, and diversify your real estate portfolio. It is also advisable to get support from real estate experts. Entrepreneurial activities are subject to various financial vulnerabilities that require attention and preparation on the part of entrepreneurs. One of the main obstacles is competition. In a competitive market, entrepreneurs face the challenge of attracting customers and distinguishing themselves from competitors. Competition can affect the profits and profitability of business activity.

Economic fluctuations pose another threat. Businesses can be affected by periods of economic recession or financial instability. A decrease in consumer demand or business expenditure can jeopardize the financial viability of a company.

Improper financial management is another threat that can undermine the financial balance of the business. Difficulties in balancing income and expenses, lack of liquidity, or excessive debt can lead to serious financial problems.

Challenges in personnel management can rap-present a financial threat. Costs related to staff recruitment, training, and compensation can in-crease the company's budget. In addition, litigation or disputes with employees can result in unexpected costs. Dependence on a few customers or suppliers is another aspect to consider. If a company relies on a limited number of customers or suppliers, a change in their circumstances can have a significant impact on the company's business.

Technological innovation and changes in the sect-ore can pose threats as well as opportunities. Businesses must be able to adapt to new trends and technologies to remain competitive. Failure to do so can jeopardize the survival of the enterprise. To protect business operations from financial threats, it is important to adopt sound management practices. These include careful financial planning, diversification of revenue sources, prudent management of personnel, and continual search for growth opportunities. Access to professional legal and financial advice can help entrepreneurs make informed decisions and mitigate financial risks.

We conclude our analysis of the risks to which assets in their various forms are potentially exposed by dealing with personal assets. One of the main threats is their devaluation. Over time, some assets such as vehicles may lose value, affecting the potential for resale or use as collateral for loans. Accidents and accidental damage are another threat, which can lead to unforeseen expenses for repairs or replacements.

To mitigate these financial threats to personal assets, it is critical to take a prudent and planned approach. This includes assessing the necessary insurance cover, setting up an emergency fund, responsible financial management and covering excessive debt.

## Succession planning

Succession planning is an often-underestimated aspect of financial protection, especially for those who have recently entered the working population. Many young people view this practice as something to be addressed only in the very distant future, associating it primarily with the elderly. This mindset, if-well spread, can pose significant risks to both their assets and the financial stability of their families.

Several reasons underlie this reluctance. Basically, it is common to focus on current situations, prompting us to prioritize immediate goals, such as professional growth or buying a house, relegating estate planning to the background. Add to this the feeling of invulnerability, often associated with youth, which can lead to procrastination of succession planning until reaching a more advanced fa-se of life.

Some may not feel it is important to plan for succession because they may not yet possess enough assets to justify the cost. In addition, they may not be aware of the options available and the importance of succession planning. In some situations, fear of dealing with certain issues could be a reason for neglecting estate planning, as it involves complex discourses about death and the division of assets.

While considering the factors mentioned above, the threats to financial wealth related to succession cannot be overlooked, given their relevance within the entire financial landscape. Without a valid will or proper estate planning, accumulated assets may be subject to laws and regulations that may not reflect the intentions of the deceased. This can result in increased tax burdens or, even, divisions of assets that do not re-specify the individual's wishes.

In addition, succession issues can lead to disputes among family members, creating tensions and emotional uncertainties. This can not only have an impact on financial wealth, but also on the relationship between family members. It is therefore vital, even for a young person, to consider succession planning as an integral part of overall financial management. Drawing up a will, identifying beneficiaries, assessing tax implications and clearly communicating one's wishes to family members can help ensure that the transfer of assets is smooth and consistent with the person's objectives.

Protecting your money is not just a precautionary measure, but a vital step in ensuring your long-term financial security. Making informed decisions, creating a financial cushion, exploring insurance options, diversifying investments, and succession planning are all ways to build a strong financial shield.

Chapter 6

# How to grow money

We are approaching the conclusion of our journey. Up to this point, we have carefully examined the fundamental concepts related to the management of finances. We have covered topics ranging from expense discipline to the concept of savings, from financial planning to asset protection, and we have discussed the importance of avoiding the accumulation of debt.

Every single action taken so far has played a key role in laying the foundation for your financial future. However, it is time to expand the boundaries of your financial knowledge, going beyond simply managing your day-to-day finances and opening the way to new levels of possibilities.

Saving is an essential step toward realizing our financial goals, but we must remember that some larger goals require a broader approach. It is not enough to simply set aside a portion of our earnings; we must also explore investment options, consider acquiring financial skills, and sometimes even seek opportunities for professional growth.

Achieving goals such as buying a house or a luxury car requires a strategic, planned vision that embraces not only the preservation of money, but also its growth and the optimization of the financial resources at our disposal. In this way, we can maximize the likelihood of realizing our dreams, gradually moving closer to what we wish to achieve.

To better understand this challenge, suppose you want to buy a car and assume that your dream car costs about 50,000 dollars. If you decided to re-spend a fixed portion of your salary, you could re-set aside 500 dollars per month. However, it would take more than 100 months, equivalent to more than 8 years, to be able to raise sufficient funds to purchase car. Honestly, this period would be excessively long, even for those with inexhaustible patience. And all this is without considering the inevitable increase in prices over time!

The combination of savings and investment is the key to solving the problem, allowing one to approach the desired goal faster and more efficiently. The main type of investment is represented by stocks. Investing in shares represents more than just a financial transaction; it is a direct involvement in a company's path to success and challenges. Being a shareholder means sharing in the company's fortunes and misfortunes: when the value of the stock rises, investors can profit from it; likewise, they can receive periodic dividends. However, stocks are inherently volatile and risky, as their value can fluctuate note-ably depending on market conditions and corporate pre-stations.

For those who prefer a slightly lower degree of risk, bonds represent a possibility that should be carefully evaluated.

These debt securities, issued by governments or corporations, function as a loan contract with investors. In return for their investment, investors receive periodic interest and repayment of principal at maturity. However, the performance of bonds is also affected by market conditions and interest rates, and there are issuer-related risks that could affect the ability to repay.

In this context, mutual funds are an attractive alternative. By aggregating capital from different investors, mutual fund managers create a diversified portfolio, often consisting of a combination of stocks and bonds. This diversification reduces the risk associated with a single security but does not eliminate it completely. Management fees and returns can vary depending on the fund.

ETFs, which trade on the stock exchange like stocks, sequence a similar model to mutual funds, but offer greater liquidity and flexibility. However, risks re-main related to market volatility.

Once it is understood that each type of investment presents unique opportunities and risks, the decision regarding the path to take will depend on personal financial preferences and the ability to manage related challenges. One pillar of creating a balanced portfolio is diversification among different asset classes, such as equities and obligations. This distribution helps mitigate the risk associated with a single investment, as each type of as-set reacts differently to market fluctuations.

Another tactic is to divide the portfolio among different industry sectors and geographic regions. This approach aims to prevent excessive focus on a single area, so as to mitigate the effects of possible turbulence that might affect particular sectors. A diversified distribution provides a kind of additional protection in circumstances where certain parts of the market might face periods of uncertainty.

It is also essential to consider the temporal horizon of investments. Short-term goals re-require a more cautious approach than long-term goals, which might benefit from a bit more volatility to achieve higher returns.

Portfolio maintenance is an equally critical aspect. Markets are constantly evolving, and assets that look promising today may not be as profitable tomorrow. Constantly monitoring investment performance and re-balancing the portfolio periodically is a wise practice to maintain alignment with goals and desired risk. By exploiting these insights and adapting them to one's own situation, one can build a portfolio that can meet the challenges and seize the opportunities of the investment world.

## Long-term investments

The frenzy of current events may push you to seek huge gains, but it is in long-term investments that you will find your way to amazing results. What makes them so attractive is their ability to multiply your money over time.

When you allocate your funds in growth-oriented investments over the long term, you start a process in which your capital begins to work to your advantage. You do not need to be a financial expert to increase your potential. What is needed is just patience; it is like planting a tree that grows and bears fruit over the years, offering a bountiful harvest. Time and patience will liberate the incredible power of compound interest.

Let's take an example that is sure to capture your imagination: suppose you invest 1,000 dollars at a compound interest rate of 5 percent per year. After the first year, you will earn 50 dollars in interest, bringing the total to 1,050 dollars. But this is where the magic kicks in: on the second year, you will earn interest not only on the initial 1,000 dollars, but also on the 50 dollars of interest earned the previous year. This means that in the second year you will earn 52.50 dollars in interest, bringing the total to 1,102.50 dollars. And so on, the money keeps multiplying, increasing more and more. Compound interest is like a financial engine that accelerates as time passes.

The earlier you start, the more you will have the magic factor of exponential growth on your side. You might initially underestimate the effect, but over time, compound interest reveals its power in surprising ways, even doubling your capital in a shorter time than you think.

The key difference between simple interest and compound interest is that the former generates a constant gain based on the initial capital, while the latter multiplies the gain by including previously earned interest. The beauty of compound interest is that it works regardless of the initial amount. Even modest sums can grow amazingly over time if given a chance to work their magic. This concept is an invitation to think big even starting with small amounts.

Think about how powerful this force can be when combined with your ability to save regularly. Each additional contribution to your initial investment becomes like a new seed you plant, ready to grow and thrive. Compound interest is a financial engine that accelerates over time, creating exponential growth that can bring you closer and closer to your financial goals.

In addition, long-term investments allow you to manage market fluctuations in a more tranquil way. When you have a broad time horizon, you have the privilege of allowing the market to fluctuate between its moments of growth and decline, without impacting your investments, which can continue to grow steadily.

Warren Buffett, one of the world's most famous investors, built his fortune through long-term investing. He bought shares in solid companies and kept them in his portfolio for decades. Over the years, the companies prospered, and the value of its shares grew exponentially. This did not happen overnight, but through a patient and mi-rated approach over time.

Another example is that of Peter Lynch, a well-known mutual fund geo-store. He has shown how long-term investing in companies that produce goods and services that people always need can lead to significant returns. He has taken positions in sectors co-equal with technology and consumption and has held his positions as companies grew and expanded over the years. In addition, there are stories of ordinary people who have invested in index funds, which track the general performance of the stock market. These investors benefited from the positive market trend in the long term without having to make complicated choices. They took advantage of the multiplier effect of compound interest to see their savings grow over the years.

These examples show that long-term investment can make a difference in building wealth. It is not a matter of looking for the next "hot" investment, but of building a solid foundation over time. It is not necessary to be a stockbroker or have huge sums of money. When it comes to investing, constancy and perseverance are often more important than immediate choices.

So, think big, start early, and let time do its work to turn your investments into a long-term success story.

## Real estate and property

The acquisition of tangible assets such as houses, commercial space or land offers the opportunity to generate income through renting and to benefit from value appreciation over time. However, it is important to recognize that this strategy involves some unique challenges compared to the alternative of investing in equities.

In real estate investing, one of the crucial elements is the operational management of properties. Real estate investors must deal with issues co-equal with finding reliable tenants, maintaining properties regularly, and managing any issues that may arise. Unlike investing in stocks, where the investor can simply buy and hold stocks, real estate investing requires an ongoing commitment to monitoring and managing properties.

In addition, investing in real estate often requires a significant investment and can involve additional expenses such as maintenance, taxes, and as-sureties. Real estate investment also has an important social impact; by providing housing or commercial space that people want, your investments could help develop the community. This aspect could give an added sense of fulfilment to your per-course in real estate.

## Entrepreneurship and startups

Entrepreneurial activity, when guided by a so-lid vision and a determination to realize your dreams, can become an effective means of multiplying capital in surprising ways, turning creativity into tangible profits. This fascinating journey often starts with an innovative idea, fueled by passion and the belief that it can make a difference in the business world.

However, the path is not without challenges. Financial uncertainty, fierce competition and the need to face unforeseen obstacles can discourage even the boldest would-be entrepreneurs. But it is precisely through challenge and adaptation that the financial management and entrepreneurial skills that ultimately lead to success can be developed.

An essential element in achieving financial success in entrepreneurship lies in the ability to learn from experiences and mistakes. Obstacles can prove to be real valuable lessons re: the market, financial management, and innovation. Failure should not be interpreted as an end, but rather as a stage along the way that opens the door to an opportunity for reflection, reworking, and refinement of one's strategy.

The ability to have complete control over finances, which goes beyond simply managing profits and extends to the freedom to make decisions about how to invest and reinvest earnings, is one of the main van- vantages associated with starting a business. Entrepreneurs can adopt personalized investment strategies, choosing to diversify their portfolios or expand into new promising areas so as to increase their chances of success.

Finally, starting a business can enable youth to maximize their potential. They can express their creativity, embrace the challenge of co-building something of their own, and develop a distinctive entrepreneurial identity. This process can instill confidence and self-discipline, skills that go far beyond business and can positively influence other aspects of life.

A different option than starting one's own business is to invest in other businesses, without having to actively participate. This technique offers the opportunity to participate in the success of businesses without having to deal with the problems of day-to-day operations. In contrast to buying shares in the stock market, which often involves an impersonal relationship with the company, investing in real companies in-ducts a tangible and more direct connection. Such investment is based on the sharing of capital, a participation that is not limited to the value of the shares but reflects a genuine commitment to the company itself.

The investor, in this scenario, acts as a financial partner. This role does not imply the direct assumption of operational or decision-making responsibilities. The investor is not involved in the day-to-day management of the company but works side-by-side with the founders and managers to support the growth and achievement of the company's goals.

The prospect of investing in real companies opens the door to an in-depth understanding of business challenges and opportunities. Participatory investors can offer strategic advice, network valuable resources, and share key expertise. This contributes to the well-being of the company and the creation of a supportive ecosystem. This investment philosophy is therefore based on the idea of collaboration and partnership. The investor is not a passive spectator, but an actor who contributes attentively to the company's journey. This approach establishes a deeper and more engaging relationship, characterized by a sense of accomplishment that goes beyond mere financial return. However, it is critical to recognize that this form of investment requires careful evaluation of the companies in which one invests. Diligent research and critical analysis are essential to identify opportunities that align with one's goals and skills. The choice of partner companies is crucial to ensuring a successful investment.

## Passive income

The prospect of passive income, with its promises of earning money without the need for constant commitment, is an idea that captures the imagination of many.

However, it is crucial to understand that this is not a shortcut to getting rich quick, but rather an ongoing commitment to building sustainable sources of income over time.

If you are willing to learn, challenge yourself, and adapt to the challenges you encounter along the way, you may find that investing in passive income can offer opportunities for personal and financial growth that go beyond expectations.

The key aspect of passive income is its ability to work for you 24/7, allowing you to enjoy the fruits of your labor even when you are not actively involved. However, the widespread belief that passive income is completely commitment-free is completely unfounded. It is true that, once set in motion, it can require less effort than traditional work, but initial initiative and dedication are essential. It is not a choice between actively working or enjoying an idle rich life. It is an opportunity that requires a balance between the investment of energy and the benefit of greater financial freedom.

Passive income can offer a diversified lifestyle, but active and forward-looking commitment is required to achieve it. Here are some examples of sources of passive income:

- **Real estate rentals**: Owning real estate property for rent can generate passive income in the form of monthly rents from tenants.

- **Stock dividends**: Investing in stocks of companies that pay dividends allows you to receive periodic income based on your ownership share.

- **Interest from financial investments**: Investing in bonds, certificates of deposit or other financial instruments can generate income in the form of interests.

- **Income from online affiliation**: Participation in affiliate programs on online platforms allows you to earn a percentage of the sales generated through your affiliate links.

- **Royalty from intellectual property**: If you own music, books, software or other creative products, you can earn royalties every time someone buys or uses your intellectual property.

- **Franchise income**: Owning a franchise allows you to earn a portion of the profits generated from your unit's activities.

- **Life insurance annuity**: Some life insurance policies include a savings component that can generate periodic annuities over the years.

- **Real estate fund investments**: Participation in real estate funds allows one to benefit from the returns of real estate investments without having to manage the properties directly.

- **Income from content creation**: Creating valuable online content, such as YouTube videos, blogs or podcasts, can generate income through advertising, sponsorships and donations from your fans.

- **Rental income**: Renting equipment, vehicles or other assets can generate passive income from renters' pay checks.

Remember that each source of passive income has its own benefits and risks, so again it is important to do thorough re-search and evaluate opportunities based on your skills, resources, and financial goals.

## Opportunities in the digital world

Opportunities to invest and generate returns in the digital world present themselves as fertile ground for those seeking innovative opportunities in today's ever-changing economic landscape.

This space, characterized by rapid change and constant technological innovation, offers various avenues for creating financial value. One of the most promising areas is electronic commerce. With the rise of online shopping and the increasing adoption of e-commerce, investing in digital platforms can prove to be a lucrative business. By creating virtual stores, optimizing the user experience and using online marketing strategies, you can reach a wide audience and increase profits. You can sell physical or digital pro-ducts through your online store, automatizing much of the sales and shipping process. Although it requires some initial work to set up and run the shop, once started it can generate revenue while you sleep.

In parallel, the world of cryptocurrencies and blockchain has catalyzed the attention of investors and enthusiasts. The volatility of cryptocurrencies can represent an opportunity for experienced traders, while the underlying technology, the blockchain, offers innovative solutions for data and transaction management. Investment in blockchain-related projects could prove to be a game changer for those seeking a cutting-edge approach.

Social media platforms offer another channel for investing and generating profits. Imagine having a blog or YouTube channel dedicated to a passion of yours that constantly attracts the attention of an interested audience. Over time, you could monetize your content through advertising, sponsorships or sales of related products.

Digital advertising, influenced by huge reach and precise audience segmentation, allows you to pro-promote products and services in a targeted way. Investment in marketing strategies on these platforms can have a significant impact on a brand's positioning and visibility.

In addition, technological innovation has given rise to the financial technology or "fintech" sector. This area is characterized by a range of new financial tools and services, including digital payments, peer-to-peer lending, and automated investment management. Investing in fintech start-ups can provide an opportunity to be part of a revolution in the financial industry.

## Plan your financial path

In an age of advanced technologies and accessible financial resources, the expectation of rapid earnings can drive people to seek quick fixes to improve their financial situation. However, it is crucial to understand that successful financial management re-requires a well-thought-out approach and a long-term vision.

It is unrealistic to expect to achieve extraordinary gains overnight or with impulsive investments. Instead, it must be understood that the true fruits of financial commitment can only be reaped over time.

The various get-rich-quick strategies that promise quick and exorbitant returns are ephemeral solutions that do not take into account long-term financial stability. We often find ourselves reading advice on how best to manage our money and achieve financial stability. But it is not enough just to acquire theoretical knowledge; it is crucial to translate it into concrete actions. It is not only a matter of knowing what to do, but also of having the will to act and actively pursue your goals.

Imagine if you learned all the best techniques in the investment world or had a solid foundation in savings, but then stood still without ever putting these skills into practice. You would get no benefit from your accumulated financial wisdom.

So, I challenge you to go beyond just a theoretical understanding of personal finance and apply it in rea-le life. Learn to plan your monthly budget, save a percentage of your income regularly, and carefully examine investment opportunities as they arise.

Investing in your continuing professional education by accumulating specialized knowledge in your field of interest can lead to increased career opportunities and, consequently, increased earnings over time. In addition, it is important to consider di-versification of investments as a key element in protecting one's assets. Not putting all your eggs in one financial basket might seem trivial, but it is often overlooked. By diversifying investments among different asset classes (such as stocks, bonds, or real estate), you reduce the overall risk of your portfolio and increase your chances of stable returns over the long term.

Finally, I stress the importance of perseverance in the pursuit of financial growth. There will be inevitable ups and downs along the way to one's financial goals. But remember that every obstacle overcome will make you stronger and more determined to achieve your goals.

Next, don't forget the importance of continuous learning in personal finance. Read books, attend seminars or consult qualified professionals to expand your financial knowledge. This constant quest for information will help you adapt to changing economic conditions and make more informed decisions

# Chapter 7

# Ten final tips

When we talk about financial habits and their influence on our lives, it is crucial to understand that the focus should not be limited only to the result, but we should put special emphasis on the importance of steering our lives in the right direction.

Financial habits play an extraordinary role through their daily constancy and commitment. This gradual and steady approach has the power to generate outstanding results that can profoundly transform our financial well-being over time. They should not be regarded as a magic wand to achieve instant financial success, but rather as modest bricks that, put together with care and dedication, build a solid and lasting structure. This is the reason why it is crucial to adopt these habits as early as possible, to give this "structure" time to grow and consolidate.

The cumulative effect of healthy financial habits is what can really make a difference in the long run. When we start saving a percentage of our income on a regular basis, we are creating a habit that instructs us to live within our possibilities. This not only allows us to set aside savings, but also teaches us to take responsibility for our financial situation.

Good financial habits are not just about saving money. It is also about managing expenses prudent, avoiding the accumulation of debt and making informed investment decisions. When we adopt the habit of planning and following a monthly budget, we are developing a fundamental skill for managing our finances effectively.

It is important to start early, ideally from a young age, because time is a crucial factor in the world of finances. Compound interest works in our favour when we save and invest over the long term. Every day you don't adopt good financial habits is a lost opportunity to grow your money.

I) **Invest in assets, challenge liabilities** - The first good financial practice to embrace is to focus on positive financial resources, so-called assets, and limit situations that involve costs (liabilities). An asset is something that has value and/or brings money into your pocket because it generates income and/or cash flow. In contrast, all those situations that involve money going out of your pocket and incurring expenses to you are considered liabilities. In the broadest sense, an asset is something value that you own and that ideally increases your financial resources because it generates income and/or cash flow.

Financial assets are true strategic allies in managing your wealth. They play a dual role: on the one hand, they allow you to plan savings for the future; on the other, they generate returns that contribute to increasing the overall value of your assets. Over time then, assets tend to increase their intrinsic value, going beyond the mere generation of cash flow. This steady appreciation can contribute to the growth of your assets, as you can leverage the gain from the sale of the assets themselves.

Take, for example, the purchase of a house to put to income. Initially you may have to invest a considering sum, but this expense is actually an investment in a more secure future: not only do you forfeit the rent, but you also have the opportunity to see the value of your property grow over the years. Similarly, financial investments, such as stocks or bonds, can generate passive income streams over time, in the form of dividends and coupons, turning your savings into earnings.

On the other hand, there are liabilities that, in obvious ways, hinder your financial interests by absorbing your resources through expenses. Take the example of a luxury car. These high-end vehicles are consciously known for their exclusive design, exceptional performance, and luxurious interior. They are often produced by prestigious automakers and are intended for a highly affluent clientele. These cars are not only means of transportation, but also represent status symbols and objects of desire for car enthusiasts and collectors. Although they can bring prestige and personal pleasure to the owner, it is important to carefully consider the long-term financial impact of owning and operating a luxury car.

From a personal finance perspective, such cars are generally considered liabilities. This is because their purchase represents a significant expense involving ongoing costs such as maintenance, insurance, taxes and depreciation in value over time. That car that looked like an investment turns out invested to be an ongoing expense, a liability that eats away at your resources instead of building them up.

Understanding the distinction between assets and liabilities re-plays a crucial role in making illuminous financial decisions and wise choices. In short, the secret to boosting your financial health lies in recognizing which side of the scale you are operating on. Assets are the trusted companions that work in your favour and generate positive outcomes. On the contrary, liabilities, although they may seem attractive at first, will end up leaving you in a more disadvantageous financial situation than initially.

II) **Stabilize your standard of living** - Increased income is undoubtedly an exciting prospect, as it offers the chance to elevate your lifestyle and fulfil long-postponed desires. However, it is important to consider one crucial aspect. By immediately adapting your lifestyle to your new income level, you deprive yourself of a valuable opportunity: the chance to greatly expand your financial freedom.

This is the ideal time to maintain financial stability. If you are already living well with your current lifestyle, there is no need to seek unnecessary luxuries. Of course, indulging in small gratifications is legitimate and healthy, but the point is to avoid an uncontrolled growth in expenditure that exceeds real needs. Instead, consider adopting a reverse strategy: keep your costs stable while your income increases. This practice would allow you to increase your savings, which can then be allocated to meet unexpected expenses or to invest in profitable opportunities. These could include buying property, starting a business or creating an investment portfolio. In addition, such financial resources could be valuable in emergency situations, such as unexpected medical expenses or job loss.

In addition, the benefit of avoiding a rapid rise in one's lifestyle is that one could habituate to manage a higher income efficiently. This adjustment period can be an opportunity to optimize one's budget strategy by prioritizing and carefully evaluating each expense. Learning to maximize the value of each dollars spent, seeking savings opportunities, and investing in a targeted manner become key elements in ensuring lasting financial stability. Finally, maintaining consistency in spending not only helps build a solid financial foundation, but also helps reduce stress and anxiety related to financial fluctuations. Hasty decisions to change lifestyle can lead to a cycle of increasing costs, which over time can become difficult to maintain.

III) **Do Not Compare Yourself** - We often feel the temptation to measure ourselves against those who have already achieved the financial success we aspire to, hoping to steal some hidden secret from them. However, this practice can often generate insecurities and dissatisfaction instead of inspiration sought.

Observing those who are at a more advanced stage in achieving financial prosperity can make us feel inadequate and lagging expectations. However, it is important to recognize that their journey is unique and cannot be compared to ours. They had an advantage of time and opportunity that we may not yet have had. They began their financial journey in a different context, at a different time, and with different resources. Their success can and should be a source of inspiration, but it should not be used as an evaluative tool.

We can study the strategies and paths that led to their success and apply them to our personal circumstances and financial goals. This process allows us to set clearer, more concrete goals for our financial future and discover new ways to improve the management of our finances.

Instead of passively allowing ourselves to be influenced, we can intelligently exploit benchmarks, using them as a stimulus to achieve new financial goals. As you create your own path, be inspired by the triumphs of others and model them on your own unique situation. Observing what is achievable can fuel your aspirations, but it is fundamental to maintain a realistic and patient attitude, always keeping in mind that your path is individual and valuable. In any progress, recognize its value and maintain motivation in overcoming challenges to achieve your goals.

IV) **Don't neglect the importance of taxes** - Taxes are a fundamental pillar of society, supporting public services and infrastructure that contribute to the collective well-being, and it is important to recognize their role in building and maintaining a fair and efficient community.

However, the influence of taxes on personal finances is significant. Tax rates, deductions and credits can have a considerable impact on the amount of money that ultimately reaches our pockets.

Understanding the different tax regimes and deductions can help you optimize your financial situation. The most interesting aspect is that taxes are not stable: tax laws may change, deductions may vary, and new policies may emerge. It is vital, therefore, to stay informed about new regulations and take advantage of opportunities as they arise.

Fortunately, there are several strategies and solutions that can help you pay less tax in a way that is tax-related and compliant. Using tax deductions, tax credits, and other smart strategies, income tax, property taxes, sales taxes, and other forms of taxation can be reduced.

Medical expenses, for example, can be subject to tax credits or tax deductions. Keep track of medical expense incurred and be sure to take advantage of all available tax benefits. This can include expenses for doctor visits, medications, therapies, health insurance and more. Education expenses, such as tuition, textbooks and vocational training courses, may also be subject to tax deductions or tax credits.

However, in a complex and continuing tax landscape, the best approach is often to work with experienced tax and financial planning professionals. Turning to qualified tax advisors can provide the confidence to make informed decisions and optimize one's tax situation. Specialized consulting can be an invaluable guide in expecting different options and choosing the most appropriate strategies to reduce one's tax burden and preserve one's financial well-being over the long term.

V) **Adopt a positive mindset** - Adopting a positive mental attitude in personal finances is crucial to creating a solid foundation for financial success. Our mind plays a key role in shaping our financial actions and decisions. A positive outlook pushes us to see challenges as opportunities for growth, motivates us to seek innovative solutions, and permits us to face difficulties with determination rather than fear.

Financial optimism motivates us to plan with confidence and pursue ambitious goals. It encourages us to learn from mistakes, rather than become discouraged, and to remain focused on long-term goals. A positive mental attitude makes us more resilient in the face of financial uncertainties, enabling us to adapt to changes and face difficult times with hope.

In addition, financial optimism affects our relationship with money. It helps us develop healthy and responsible financial habits, avoiding impulsive or negative-emotion-based behaviors. This attitude also pro- motes an open mindset toward learning and acquiring financial skills, enabling us to make more informed and thoughtful decisions.

But this positive mindset is not simply an exercise in imagination; it is a powerful lever that can make the difference between a difficult path and a satisfying one. Imagine you have a magnifying glass in your mind: If you focus your attention on financial problems, they will inevitably grow out of proportion. Instead, if you direct your gaze toward solutions, you open previously hidden doors. Focusing on what you can do, rather than on what seems impossible, changes the game.

This isn't just motivational talk: there's hard evidence of the effect of mindset on your financial situation. Studies show that those who maintain a positive mindset tend to make more thoughtful financial decisions, cope better with challenges, and even improve their re- spending and investment skills.

VI) Building a good credit rating is one of the fundamental pillars of personal finance, directly impacting the ability to access loans and financing. This numerical score, also known as a credit score or credit score, reflects your reliability in managing credit and debt. Financial institutions and creditors use it as an indicator to assess the risk associated with you as a borrower and decide whether to lend to you and on what terms.

High creditworthiness is synonymous with financial responsibility. It shows that you have a track record of paying bills on time, managing credit cards wisely, and meeting financial commitments. This translates into tangible benefits. When you have a good credit score, you are more likely to get loans at lower interest rates. This means that, in the long run, you will pay less interest on the money borrowed, which can mean considerable savings.

On the other hand, a low credit score can comport financial obstacles. If you have a poor credit score, you may be considered a higher risk by lenders, and you may struggle to obtain financing or pre-lending. Even if you are granted loans, interest rates will often be higher, increasing the total cost of borrowing over time. In addition, a low credit score could limit your ability to rent an apartment, obtain a credit card, or even get a job, as some employers may require a credit control as part of the selection process.

Maintaining optimal creditworthiness requires a judicious approach to credit management. This means avoiding accumulating excessive debt, paying bills on time, maintaining responsible use of credit cards, and not exceeding credit limits. Monitoring your creditworthiness regularly allows you to spot any errors or fraudulent activity and deal with them promptly.

Taking care, then, of your creditworthiness is an important step toward building a solid financial base and the ability to achieve your financial goals. Again, consultations with financial experts can help you better understand how to mi-improve your creditworthiness and make the most of the financial opportunities available to you.

VII) **Do charity** - Charity plays a significant role in personal finance, as it provides an opportunity to contribute to the community and improve one's financial situation through donations and solidarity actions. Although it may seem counter-intuitive to consider charitable giving as part of personal financial management, it can positively influence several aspects of an individual's financial life.

First, charity can help cultivate a sense of gratitude and awareness with respect to one's financial resources. Donating to social causes, charitable organizations, and humanitarian initiatives can make one reflect on the fact that one has resources that others may not have, encouraging a more responsible approach to personal spending and saving. This can lead to wiser financial decisions and greater care in affronting unnecessary expenditures.

Second, charitable giving can offer tax advantages. Donations to recognized charitable organizations can be deducted from taxes, reducing the overall tax burden. This can be a way to optimize your personal tax situation while at the same time supporting causes that you consider important. In addition, charitable giving can help create a wider social network. Participating in charitable and volunteer efforts allows you to connect with people with similar interests and develop meaningful relationships. These connections can also be beneficial from a professional and personal point of view, opening up opportunities for new encounters, knowledge exchange and possible collaborations.

Finally, charity can bring personal satisfaction and a sense of purpose. Helping to improve the lives of others and solve social problems can provide a sense of accomplishment and well-being that goes beyond the financial dimension. This emotional well-being can positively affect mental health and overall quality of life.

VIII) **Networking** - Building a strong network of relationships is not just a tactic for success, but a strategy that opens the door to opportunities never imagined.

The opportunity to connect with influential people in business and investment is a treasure not to be underestimated. These relationships can act as sources of support, provide you with valuable advice, and even open doors to business opportunities that may be beyond your expectations.

Imagine having the opportunity to learn directly from business professionals, to receive advice from those who have already been through the challenges you are facing. The right connections can offer you a different perspective, open your eyes to new ways of thinking and acting, and ultimately accelerate your path to financial success.

Cultivating relationships is not only about what you can receive, but also what you can give. Sharing-your know-how, experiences, and time with others creates a mutual flow of benefits. These connections are not only based on financial interests, but also on-sharing values, visions, and goals. These relationships can help you grow not only financially, but also personally and professionally. The opportunity to build a strong network of contacts is an investment that pays unexpected dividends over time. The right connections can open doors that would otherwise remain closed and can be the boost you need to overcome challenges and achieve success. Working to build a network of influential relationships is a strategy that cannot be underestimated, as the strength of a network can be a powerful catalyst in shaping your financial future.

IX) **Always live by your scale of values** - Adopting an attitude congruent with your personal values is a highly valuable behavior to embrace from young adulthood. This means respecting personal financial priorities without the need for justification, avoiding comparisons with others or feelings of obligation to neighbors or long-time friends. Think of your value scale as an in-tern compass, a beacon that illuminates the path to your financial dreams and goals. This personal guide gives you the guidance you need to make financial decisions in li-ne with your authenticity and desires.

It's easy to get carried away by social pressure or the expectations of others about what a successful vice should look like. But remember that financial success should never be defined by what others think or do. Your happiness and financial security depend on your authenticity in pursuing goals that resonate with you, that reflect your deepest values and aspirations.

Embarking on this path, it is only natural to want to acquire advice and learn from those who have already travelled similar paths. Yet, it is critical to approach this advice with a personal filter based on your own values and goals. Consulting experts and seeking advice is certainly a wise step but let us never forget to listen to the inner voice, the one that reflects the values that define who we are and where we want to go in our financial choices. It is an equilibrium between the wisdom of others and our own inner intuition.

When you take financial actions based on your scale of values, there is a sense of authenticity and integrity that comes with you. Your confidence increases as you know you are al-lined with what is truly important to you. And this can positively affect every aspect of your life, not just finances. Consistency between your values and your financial actions creates a sense of inner peace and satisfaction that goes beyond the numbers on a bank account.

X) **Cultivate gratitude** - Developing an attitude of recognition and appreciation for the positive things in life, including the financial aspects, involves reflecting regularly on what you have, and the opportunities present rather than focusing only on what is lacking.

This awareness of one's resources and small daily joys helps create a more positive and fulfilling perspective on financial management and life in general.

Immersed in a society geared toward consumerism and comparison, young people are often inclined to seek success and happiness through the accumulation of sterile material goods. In contrast, gratitude emphasizes the importance of appreciating what one has and focusing on significant life experiences beyond the material. This perspective encourages the development of a balanced and responsible financial attitude. When one embraces gratitude for the financial resources at one's disposal, one develops an inclination to carefully consider how to direct them congruently with one's values and goals. This behavior can be reflected in more thoughtful financial decisions, helping to avoid waste and unnecessary spending.

Gratitude can also create a sense of contentment and satisfaction, regardless of portfolio size. This feeling of contentment can limit the incessant pursuit of more money and material goods, which are the main sources of happiness. Instead, it can encourage the young person to seek wealth in experiences, relationships and personal growth.

These ten tips are like stars that light up the vast sky of personal finances. Each tip is a ray of wisdom, projected to guide you through the challenges and opportunities of the financial world. Remember that your financial per-course is unique, yet you share with many the re- search for stability, security and success. As you venture on this journey, keep in mind that your choices today designate the future you desire. Implement these tips carefully, adapt them to your personal context, and be patient to see the fruits of your efforts. With your goal set and an open mind, you can look to the future with confidence, knowing that you have the tools to create a solid foundation for your financial security and well-being.

# Acknowledgements

*Dear Reader,*

*Thank you from the bottom of my heart for choosing to read 'Personal Finance for Beginners'. I sincerely hope that you have found these pages informative and inspiring in your quest for more conscious financial management.*

*Your time and interest have been invaluable, and now I have a small request. If you enjoyed this book and benefited from the information shared, I kindly ask you to share your opinion by writing a review. Your words can help other readers discover the benefits of this reading and make wiser financial decisions.*

*Leaving a review is easy, and you can do so on Amazon or any other online sales portal where you purchased the book. It doesn't matter if your review is brief or detailed; what matters is your contribution to the community of readers.*

*Once again, thank you for choosing 'Personal Finance for Beginners'. Your support is invaluable, and I hope that the information contained in these pages will continue to inspire more conscious and responsible financial management in your life and the lives of others.*

*with gratitude,*

*Aidan Stanford*

Frame the QR code
with your smartphone
to **write a review**

Made in the USA
Las Vegas, NV
26 December 2023

83509906R00095